Mega Event Planning

Series Editors

Stefano Di Vita
Dipartimento Architettura Studi Urbani
Politecnico di Milano
Milano, Milano, Italy

John Lauermann
Geography
City University of New York
Cumberland, RI, USA

The Mega Event Planning Pivot series provides a global and cross-disciplinary view into the planning for the world's largest sporting, religious, cultural, and other transformative mega events. Examples include the Olympic Games, Soccer World Cups, Rugby championships, the Commonwealth Games, the Hajj, the World Youth Day, World Expositions, and parades. This series critically discusses, analyzes, and challenges the planning for these events in light of their legacies including the built environment, political structures, socio-economic systems, societal values, personal attitudes, and cultures.

Sandra Borges Tavares

Youth Policy, Citizenship Education and Olympic Games Legacies

palgrave
macmillan

Sandra Borges Tavares ⓘ
Research Centre for Communication and Culture (CECC)
Catholic Portuguese University
Lisbon, Portugal

ISSN 2633-5859 ISSN 2633-5867 (electronic)
Mega Event Planning
ISBN 978-981-99-6578-6 ISBN 978-981-99-6579-3 (eBook)
https://doi.org/10.1007/978-981-99-6579-3

This Palgrave Macmillan imprint is published by the registered company Springer Nature Singapore Pte Ltd.
The registered company address is: 152 Beach Road, #21-01/04 Gateway East, Singapore 189721, Singapore

If disposing of this product, please recycle the paper.

To Afonso and Vasco

Acknowledgements

This book is above all the result of the efforts put forward by the young people who were willing to take part in this research. Throughout the process of meeting and interviewing them, I was asked many times about the outcome and whether they would be able to read some of it or see anything published about their contributions. Thus, this is also part of their legacy. I thank them for their time and for sharing their valuable experiences and contributions.

I am also indebted to the people I met along the way, who opened doors for contacts and offered their advice, such as Miriam Pragita and António Augusto from ANDI, Mário Volpi from UNICEF, Regina Assis, Gizele Martins, Ana Paula da Silva and Leandro Paz. A very special thank you to Paulo Lima, a friend and activist from Viração, esteemed Professor David Buckingham, Professor Anna Reading and Dr Jessica Rapson. A big thank you to my friend and colleague Luís Pereira who was and still is a guiding shoulder whenever advice is needed.

Finally, I thank all my family, in particular my mother Cesaltina Borges Tavares, and my husband Luís Manso for their love and support.

CONTENTS

LIST OF FIGURES

LIST OF TABLES

CHAPTER 1

Youth Citizenship and the (In)tangible Legacies of the Olympic Games

Abstract This introductory chapter addresses and explores an important gap in the mega-events literature considered critical to understanding and advancing research on youth civic participation, citizenship and youth policy. It does so by exploring and critiquing existing scholarship on young people's past, future and present perceptions of the Olympics taking place in their cities, particularly drawing on the two case studies used in the study—London 2012 and Rio 2016 Olympic Games. It develops from the view of youth as a target group, mainly by political and governmental bodies responsible for the planning of highly mediatised events such as the Olympic Games, and interrogates how political rhetoric is often constructed for the benefit of such entities instead of the young population. Such an approach is problematised and contested based on academic evidence that points to a lack of research on the topic, especially concerning youth policy within the Olympic Games scholarship regarding the intangible legacies of the Games. Furthermore, the chapter also explores important concepts in light of the Olympic Games, such as the importance of policy work, cultural policy and place-making, all areas that are reviewed and contemplated empirically in the context of the Olympics.

Keywords Youth • Intangible legacies • Olympics • London 2012 • Rio 2016 • Youth citizenship

© The Author(s), under exclusive license to Springer Nature Singapore Pte Ltd. 2024
S. Borges Tavares, *Youth Policy, Citizenship Education and Olympic Games Legacies*, Mega Event Planning,
https://doi.org/10.1007/978-981-99-6579-3_1

1

This book puts forward some important questions around the idea and conceptualisation of intangible legacies within mega-events and the impact they might have on the youth population and their respective settings, including how it affects and reframes their sense of citizenship. The starting point is the Summer Olympic and Paralympic Games taking place in London in 2012 and then, fast-forwarding, I look at the Rio 2016 Olympic Games, from the lenses of a diversified segment of young citizens with rights and duties. Although this book is framed around two events that took place a while ago, the empirical evidence presented here is claimed as significant to reframe youth citizenship in light of mega-events (Chatziefstathiou, 2012; Roche, 2023; Monnin, 2021).

The central argument is that little is still known about public expectations and the views of young people in relation to the event as they are often not involved in the consultations about the planning and outcomes of such events. In addition, the intersections between youth citizenship, citizenship education, cultural policy and the role of sports as a catalyst for unification or critique in these areas are brought up throughout this book as a relevant discussion in light of the Olympics and the values of Olympism. As a result, the book adds to existing works, such as on the more recent Youth Olympic Games, which although it is not the main focus of this study, the body of scholarship on this topic provides valuable insights into how young people might be engaging and relating to these types of events and how is youth perceived by the government and entities responsible for organising such events. This is done by exploring the underlying meanings of what is argued as an important gap in the mega-events literature, considered critical to understanding and advancing research in youth civic participation, citizenship and youth policy (Nordhagen, 2021; Kirakosyan, 2020; Papanikos, 2020).

I intentionally look at different time frames of the Summer Games to make sense of past, future and present perceptions of the event and in order to evaluate young people's views and insights, which brings up implications for their cities and lifestyles. However, a few references will be made to recent events, such as the Olympic Games in Tokyo 2021, and other Youth Olympic Games, as well as the more recent 2024 Olympics in Paris, in order to contextualise the arguments in line with the claims made in this book, on the impact and implications on youth citizenship and more active engagement with societies. Along the chapters, I discuss, develop and critique different perspectives about the conceptualisation of youth, especially when they are targeted by the different political and governmental bodies responsible for the planning of these highly mediatised events, such as the case of the Olympic Games. In this sense, I explore and draw upon the concept of 'youthwashing', which is a relatively new concept that suggests the recurrent use of youth images as a tool to achieve the aims or goals of some organisations or entities (Bullon-Cassis, 2024; Orsini, 2022), to connect it with some of the discourse and aims of the Olympic Games towards young people. This is done by drawing attention to how youth are often utilised by policy makers and governments as strategic 'currency' to advocate for the interests set up in these agendas, which is arguably what happens as well with such mega-events and its legacies targeted at young people. A very good recent case of this is the discourse from the 2024 Olympic Games in Paris, whose promises of a volunteering programme directed to young people and a heritage model with the view of supporting 'civic involvement, giving them more inclusive and job opportunities through the sport' is yet to be assessed and materialised (Ricordel, 2023). I also identify and explore ways through which, in some cases, the political rhetoric is constructed for the benefit of such corporate entities rather than the youth population and, as a result, the strategies and programmes that are proposed might not be the ones that would better benefit the youth population in terms of the long-lasting legacies (Bessant et al., 2024; Booth, 2024). The argument is based on the fact that many mega and global sporting events, like the Olympics or the World Cup, to give some examples, are used by the host countries and cities as an opportunity to promote a political agenda (Budiasa, 2024).

Although mega-events are one-off special events taking place at a particular time and place, they are framed in this study as an ideal opportunity for exploring youth citizenship and enactments of youth civic engagement at different levels. I claim that it is during the planning, preparation and duration of these events that the hosting cities and their locals are most affected. This is because sporting events are seen to have a profound impact on the city landscape (Doustaly & Zembri-Mary, 2024; Smith et al., 2024), as well as on citizens' sense of identity and belonging (Kazmierski-Davie & Ballouli, 2024; Misener & Mason, 2006; Owen & Chambers, 2024), let alone youth education legacies (Hwang & Henry, 2023), which in turn provides a different opportunity for local or community citizenship to actively participate in matters of their interest or voice their opinions on wider issues pertaining to society (Borges Tavares, 2022).

Aside from the Youth Olympic programme set up by the IOC, and the work already conducted on youth policy within the Olympics in general, there appears to be scarce research done so far on the intangible legacies of the Games, particularly with a focus on the youth (Seidl et al., 2021). The reason for this might be perhaps because the conceptualisation of intangible (cultural and educational) legacies is in itself complex by definition, involving what UNESCO claims as a fragile yet important aspect for 'maintaining cultural diversity in the face of globalisation' (UNESCO, n.d., n.p.). Another reason could be related to what some scholars claim in relation to the IOC legacy plans, as one aspect that it is now almost compulsory in the bidding process for hosting the Games but which in reality is seen by some scholars as a magical discourse of flattening standards of expertise to strengthen the IOC model of franchising (MacAloon, 2008).

The body of research dedicated to the impact of media events on the youth population, which includes the existing scholarship on the Olympic programmes for young people, the Youth Olympic Games and youth policy in the Olympic movement, is indeed relevant to contextualise the IOC's overall aims to mitigate this gap and advance the Olympic philosophy towards the youth population (Wong, 2011). For Hwang and Henry (2023), however, the problem with the promises of the so-called Olympism values and educational ideals set up initially by Pierre de Coubertin is that nowadays these are assessed in terms of outputs, like number of people involved in the education programmes, instead of an overview on the impact on young people's knowledge, attitudes, values and behaviour (Hwang & Henry, 2023, p. 580). In a similar vein, the work of Postlethwaite et al. (2020) on the legacy discourses of the London 2012 Olympic Games interrogates the effectiveness of the legacy plan across public, private and non-profit governing bodies with vested interests, which could be problematic for society and young people inclusive in terms of assessing the outcomes. The result of this work points to the fact that young people should be seen as a governable population, as there are many opportunities to be considered at broader societal aims in connection with young citizens. Yet, an important lacuna in academic contributions from a youth-centric approach to media, mega-events and citizenship studies is identified and addressed in this book. To be more specific, this gap relates to what is widely claimed within the rhetoric and objectives of the International Olympic Committee (IOC) and the respective bodies involved in the organisation of the event towards the young population, in contrast with what young people themselves perceive and gain from these types of events. In other words, this book looks at the impact of the Games from the angle of young people's views and experiences of past events, by providing a space for them to voice their views and, in the process, reflect upon their citizenship values across different levels (local, national, global, transnational). The Games are therefore used as a catalyst for debating questions and themes linked to youth citizenship. The approach proposed here, which intersects different theoretical fields and epistemological areas, is claimed as not been researched in great depth. As a result, it presents an excellent opportunity to contribute with original data and findings towards a better understanding of youth policy work and the legacy of mega-events like the Olympics, both theoretical and methodologically for other research projects around mega sporting events.

The empirical work for this research took place in two cities where the Summer Olympic and Paralympic Games happened (London 2012 and Rio 2016) yet as case studies, the methodology is developed for being used towards other similar events. The aim is to explore the extent to which such high-mediatised events might provide an opportunity for a discursive arena for young citizens to participate in and engage with their societies as an active public sphere (Arendt, 1958; Habermas, 1991) and the extent to which the programmes put together by the host cities may have a long-lasting impact on the youth population. Different levels of participation and enactments from this public are identified and aligned with the Olympics discourse on their intangible or social legacies (Cashman, 1998; Girginov, 2018; Girginov & Preuss, 2021). I am particularly interested in how these types of events are used to establish the performative role of global media in the dissemination and enactment of national identity, public opinion and citizenship, especially focused on the youth as a target group. As a result, this book explores the connotations and ideas behind the intangible legacies from the perspective of the young citizens whose cities and lives are affected, positively or negatively, by such events taking place in their settings.

In addition, an overview of how the Olympics may function as a catalyst for rich discussions on active citizenship, and national, local, transnational and cultural identity is also discussed and deconstructed given that they are relevant for thinking forward about youth policy-making in the planning of future similar events.

Alongside the analysis and theoretical considerations, I bring forward to the discussion the current scholarship and theoretical works on the conceptualisation and critiques of the Youth Olympic Games in parallel with youth policy developments with the aim of identifying areas that have already been targets of critical discussions or appraisals regarding the IOC and the Olympic movement aims for the youth.

The temporal gap between the two cases (London 2012 and Rio de Janeiro 2016) is deliberate as it offers the possibility to assess data on the participants' recollections (in the case of London) and subsequently on their 'imaginaries'[1] or expectations of the Games (which is the case of Rio de Janeiro). The aim, thus, is not to provide a comparison of these two settings or discourses, given that they are framed in terms of experiences and expectations. Instead, the purpose is to identify opportunities, problems or ideas put forward by the young participants from two global distinct contexts (Global North–South Divide), as an important contribution and data analysis for future youth policy work on the Olympic Games or any other mega-events with similar dimensions, targeting the youth population.

Hence, the excavations of participant's recollections of past events and the exploration of their imaginaries in light of the Games, taking place ahead of time, are viewed as critical aspects for these young citizens to engage with a variety of topics connected to local, national and transnational senses of identity in a critical fashion. The approach proposed here in regard to memory studies allows us to conduct an in-depth examination of young people's accounts which, in some cases its outcome, appears to contradict the messages and ideologies conveyed by the Games industry and the devised cultural and education policies targeting the younger population.

As a final note, a reminder that at the core of this study is the best interest of young people and, with that in mind, this book also hopes to contribute to the ongoing discussion on the idea of youth as a group disengaged from politics or civic participation. To that end, clear examples are provided along the book drawing from the data that suggest quite the opposite. Although this may not be representative of all young people around the world, and that is not actually the aim, the fact is that the cohort of participants who were willing to take part in this project demonstrated to be actively engaged with topics of their interest, perhaps not

---

[1] The term imaginaries is used in this context to highlight the sociological and media angle of a collective set of values, images, laws and symbols that are socially constructed by young people, in this case, as part of their imagination and expectations of the Games.

overtly in a traditional fashion, but nevertheless considered as active citizenship and participation with societal issues. Such enactments are portrayed in a non-traditional fashion, which reveals that, on the contrary to what has been suggested in some areas of youth and politics studies, young people in this study are recurrently engaging with and involved in different political agendas from a different perspective that is commonly contemplated by so-called traditional citizenship and the governments. I focus on these claims to draw attention to the role of mega-events, like the Olympics, as an important catalyst and opportunity for rethinking youth policy in terms of citizenship values within the Olympics' wider legacy plans. The case studies used in this book are from 2012 and 2016, however more recently the 2024 Olympics taking place in Paris, for example, has equally demonstrated how the youth population was contemplated in their plans and aims. One of the legacy aims of Paris Games is to make sports more accessible and beneficial for everyone, including young people, despite the various protests that took place against the bid for these Games (Bourbillères et al., 2023).

THE PERFORMATIVE ACTS OF YOUTH MEMORIES AND EXPECTATIONS

Although memory has long drawn the attention of philosophers and thinkers, it was not until the late nineteenth and early twentieth centuries that memory studies began to emerge as an important interdisciplinary field of research and popular topic for scholarly inquiry (Brown et al., 2009), prompting the interest of scholars across different disciplines, e.g. media, cultural studies, sociology and memory studies. Memory scholars in this field share the same opinion that 'memory, remembering and recording are the very key to existence, becoming and belonging' (Garde-Hansen, 2011, p. 18).

Maurice Halbwachs' (1950) seminal work on collective memory underpins part of this book's argument. By addressing memory from a sociological perspective, he claimed that memory is not an isolated, individual phenomenon but that society, too, has a memory. Also, he argued that individual memories rely upon frameworks or cadres of social memory (Halbwachs, 1950, 1992), which is an idea expanded in the case of my participants' discourses. Furthermore, Halbwachs' view that an 'individual remembers by placing himself in the perspective of the group, but one may also affirm that memory of the group realizes and manifest itself in individual memories' (Halbwachs, 1992, p. 40) is crucial for understanding identity and citizenship enactments among young people.

The idea of the media, or in this case, media events, as one of the many frameworks through which young people's experiences and memories are shaped and construed (Rigney & Erll, 2009) is claimed as significant for reframing citizenship. As a result, the cadres (or frames), stressed by Halbwach, will be transversally deployed to stress the different associations made by participants in relation to their multiple frameworks, be it social or media related, national, local or transnational. The idea of cadres of memory is explored in this book and in addition a more fluid, mediated and transnational approach is put forward. Other 'frames' are likewise considered in the examination of the participants' discourses within their personal and mediated memories or imaginaries and linked to their media consumption.

Given that the media is also an important part of this study, it feels relevant explaining the relationship between the media and memory in terms of young participants recollections and imaginaries of the Olympic Games. As a media event broadcasted to millions, the Olympic Games has a significant impact on how and why people recall certain topics, including their expectations in relation to society (Dayan & Katz, 1994; Pfister, 2013; Kohe, 2017). Media are a critical element in this process, viewed as embedded in people's mediated and mediatised experiences (Livingstone & Bober, 2005; Van Dijck, 2007; Ritchie et al., 2010).

In this book, I explore how the field of memory studies engages with different areas of media scholarship, particularly regarding mediatised sport events, like the Olympic Games, and their impact on different forms of youth experience (Roche, 2002). I support the argument that it is almost impossible to think about events of the past without discoursing about them (Garde-Hansen, 2011, p. 19), and therefore the choice of using discourse analysis as the main research method is adequate in order to 'touch upon' participants' memories and imaginations as legitimate views and opinions.

Similarly, this book supports the view that young people's experiences are partially mediated and the ubiquity of media and technologies in their lives has serious implications for how their discursive memories and imaginations are shaped and constructed. Youth discourses are therefore similarly considered from the perspective that individuals' memories are increasingly based on a past that, rather than just being remembered, is sometimes reconstructed in a current media-saturated environment (Hoskins, 2001, p. 336) and through a plethora of cultural technologies (Landsberg, 2004).

Cultural memory is equally important to underpin some expressions and enactments from the young participants. To this end, the work of Jan and Aleida Assmann (2011) is drawn upon in order to contextualise some of the approaches towards cultural memory with a focus on national identity and how societies remember.

The body of scholarship in this area connects culture and memory by analytically explaining the differences between personal, collective and cultural memory, as well as collective identity and political legitimation, all areas relevant to this book's contribution. Media events like the Olympic Games have, over the years, evolved into cultural spectacles that go beyond sports and convey important cultural and historical legacies (Shipway, 2007; Gratton et al., 2015; Garcia, 2012). In order to fully understand the implications of media events beyond sports, including the so-promised, intangible legacies, I argue that public remembrances, both at individual and collective levels, require further examination. An example of this is Article 50 of the Olympic Charter,[2] which states that no demonstration, whether political, religious or racial propaganda, is permitted in the Olympic areas. Yet, the Games have always been a favourable stage for political contestation, either by individuals, organising entities or even participating countries.[3] As this suggests, the Olympics might play a key role in the collective remembrances of citizens, representing what Assmann (2011) defines as an important part of the institutionalised and media rituals that pervade public remembrances.

As a cultural event, the Games offer a plethora of spectacles, including the now compulsory Olympic Cultural Programme set out by the IOC and organised by each host city (Garcia, 2008). Such programmes and spectacles are seen as contributing towards collective remembrances, given

---

[2] Article 50 of the Olympic Charter outlines the rules relating to advertising, demonstrations and propaganda. For more information, see https://olympics.com/athlete365/app/uploads/2020/12/Rule-50-Guidelines-Tokyo-2020.pdf.

[3] At the 1948 Olympic Games in London, known as the austerity Games, Japan and Germany were not invited since they were considered, in the aftermath of World War II, as the aggressors; China withdrew after the IOC recognised Taiwan; and Spain, Switzerland and the Netherlands boycotted the Games over the Soviet invasion of Hungary. At the 1968 Olympics in Mexico City, Tommie Smith and John Carlos performed the Black Power salute during the national anthem as a protest against racism in the USA.

that cultural memory production is a process through which 'symbolic forms must not only be preserved but also circulated and re-embodied in a society' (Assmann, 2011, p. 17). The Olympics' opening and closing ceremonies are just some examples whereby performances of the history of a nation as well as other cultural enactments are broadcasted not only to the nation but worldwide.

Theorisations of collective memory are relevant for this study as they help us contextualise the contribution of the data around youth cultural, national, local and transnational citizenship. The scholars working in this field describe collective memory by establishing a qualitative distinction between the communicative and cultural memory of individuals, which are arguably not only significant but thoroughly embedded in the participants' discourse. First, expanding on Halbwachs' social conceptualisation of collective memory—and bearing in mind the argument that memory enables us to use the past to develop a narrative of ourselves (Assmann & Czaplicka, 1995, p. 15)—the data concerning collective memory are equally contemplated in this book from a cultural rather than just a psychological or behavioural framework.

The Olympic Games offer different types of mnemonic experiences for their audiences. On the one hand, the young participants' memories are contemplated, in line with Halbwachs' view, as socially mediated and connected to a specific group. On the other hand, conversations with colleagues observed through the focus group interviews (communicative memory) provide what Assmann and Czaplicka (1995, p. 127) refer to as a 'more precise insight into the particular qualities of this everyday form of collective memory'. For instance, during the interviews with my participants, part of the discourse prompted further debate on wider issues pertaining to society, which I argue as symptomatic of an active citizenship but also is an example of communicative memory.

All in all, the connection between time, identity and memory is considered in this book across three levels: the individual, the social and the cultural (Assmann, 2011). In addition to these, the media are positioned as equally important for the conceptualisation of memory. Although Assmann's work is relevant for distinguishing between and understanding the different performative roles of cultural memory, more research is still needed to understand how cultural memory, in the context of this study, is connected to youth civic engagement and citizenship values. In the same way that Assmann and Czaplicka's (1995) critique of Halbwachs paved the way for a new conceptualisation of collective memory, the two different modi memoranda presented by these scholars (communicative and cultural memory) are elevated as interwoven and legitimate forms of remembering in light of the Olympic Games. In addition to other elements, Assmann's theory gives currency to the memories and imaginaries of young participants in relation to the Olympics. Symbols, texts and images produced as part of the Games by the participants will be contemplated as strong apparatuses and examined accordingly.

In terms of legacy of the Games, as I will discuss further in the next section, remembering and imagining are equally considered legitimate forms of legacy. It is precisely at the interstices of these two (memory and imaginary) that the work of Emily Keightley and Michael Pickering on the 'mnemonic imagination' (2012) will be useful to make sense of some of the participants' narratives and explain how they are interwoven in terms of ideas of legacy. The underlying argument of the mnemonic imagination is that memory and imagination are not considered as separate acts but instead are in a constant interstitial relationship between past and future (Keightley & Pickering, 2012, p. 42). The concept is understood as a relationship in which, while remembering, the subject (the young person) is imaginatively engaging with what is retained from the past (first- and second-hand experiences) and is continuously rearranging the 'hotchpot into relatively coherent narrative structures' (ibid., p. 43). This new conceptualisation of—and different approach to—memory and the imagination is useful for the proposed framework of youth citizenship, to understand the legacy aspects intrinsic to youth memories and imaginaries. The view that 'we draw on our memory when we imagine, but it prevents us, sometimes quite emphatically, from thinking of how we draw on our imaginations when we remember' (Keightley & Pickering, 2012, p. 45) is claimed as important to bear in mind with regard to the data analysis presented later. In other words, the discourse on remembrance is arguably anchored in imagination in the same way that imagination relies on memory, despite the temporal or settings where the empirical work took place.

Legacy, More Than Just a Buzzword?

The concept of an Olympic legacy has been debated and discussed across different fields beyond the focus on sports, by contemplating areas such as educational and cultural intangible aspects that come along with the event itself. Academically speaking, this area of research has, since 2000, been framed as an important topic in the fields of sociology of sports and events management (Chen & Henry, 2020). For these scholars, the idea of legacy is intrinsically connected with the education and cultural programmes set up by the host cities at the bidding process and throughout the whole event, which ultimately impacts upon the youth population of the host cities, too.

Yet, the idea of analysing the legacies of the Olympic Games is seen as a 'complex, wide-ranging and multi-staged process' (ibid., p. 276), particularly given the methodological nature it entails and challenges that it faces in addition to underlying theoretical limitations (ibid.). Such challenges are seen as ranging for example from a lack of longitudinal or spatial studies focused on the host cities or the nations (Chen et al., 2013; Karadakis & Kaplanidou, 2012) and a further need to identify or clarify the definition of legacy and the impact of the legacies on (both tangible and intangible) on the population in general affected by such events (Preuss, 2007).

At the core of this concept are the multiple implications that it has on people, cities, jobs, and arguably on the rise of equality and unity (McGuinness, 2015). Although the concept of mega events legacy has emerged over the last decades (Misener et al., 2013; Preuss, 2015), with an increase in the volume of publications about the legacy of the Games, there are nevertheless some gaps in research claimed in terms of identifying its conceptualisation, definitions and measurements (Scheu et al., 2021). One of the arguments around the analysis of legacy of the Olympics suggests that the empirical focus is perhaps more needed at this stage rather than a methodological one. For scholars such as Chen and Henry (2020), it appears that the use of process-tracing to understand the impact of legacy programmes related to the Games is one way forward for assessing the Olympics impact and validate internally the correlation between the legacy discourse and impact of such programmes (Chen & Henry, 2020, p. 292). The same authors also advocate for more theory-based evaluation as a promising approach to elevate not only sport policy development but also other areas inherently connected to the legacies, in policy implementation (ibid.).

In the case of this study, the multiplicity of discourses emerging from the young participants (be it local, national or transnational) are framed in this book as challenging the concept of Olympics legacy, or at least the discourse emanated from the Olympic entities and governments. At the same time, they also work as a contribution to the gap identifying in this field. In other words, I argue that such youth discourses and enactments contribute to the field, by opening discussions between legacy-programme evaluators, legacy-promise makers and policy makers in the process of determining the best way forward for youth legacies around the Olympics.

On the one hand, I focus on what is understood and defined by the Olympic Committees as intangible legacies, including the aims set out by the host countries in their bidding process, including the work already done by the Youth Olympics in bringing the best of the legacy plans for the youth. On the other hand, and by way of contrasting such views, this book explores some of the programmes put together for young people that are contended for functioning in terms of governments' interests rather than serving the young audiences (Breeze, 2009; Lenskyj, 2008). In this sense, some of the works developed by scholars such as Breeze and Kohe and Collison, respectively, on the positive role of youth philanthropy from early stages, and the critical intersection between sport organisations and commercial stakeholders, are important and need to be considered in light of the legacy plans of the Olympic Games, specifically in terms of intangible legacies addressed in programmes for youth education and active citizenship.

As such, some of the key works in this field are critiqued or expanded, by giving room to the rich data emerging from the empirical work conducted on a diverse pool of youth voices that, overall, contradict the ideologies set out by the Olympic Committee.

Legacy is thus a central theme in this book. It is also one of the most used words in the context of the Olympic Games' discourse (Torres, 2012). For some scholars, like John MacAloon (2008), the Olympic Games industry has managed to produce a legacy discourse of common and flattening standards of expertise and has strengthened the IOC's position and models of franchise with other Olympic parties (MacAloon, 2008, p. 2060). Such is the importance of this concept that, in 2002, the International Olympic Committee (IOC)[4] admitted that more research was necessary on the planning and management of legacy in the Olympics' programmes (Kaplanidou & Karadakis, 2010, p. 110), consequently launching a call for researchers to explore the role of legacies and legacy management for the Olympic host cities (ibid.). As a matter of fact, I have earlier pointed out that the understanding and conceptualisation of legacy

---

[4] The International Olympic Committee (IOC) defines Olympic Legacy as the long-term benefits created by the Games for the host city and its people during and after the Games. See further information here:

sport and mega-events still needs further revision in order to understand what entities such as the IOC and other bodies understand by legacy and how is legacy being incorporated within the education programmes for young people around the world.

While legacy is viewed as complex and multidimensional, including amongst other things the emotional constructions of the Olympic Games through the memories, rituals and symbols left behind (Cashman, 1998; Agha et al., 2012), it is also a future-oriented concept, significant for cultural and social policy, including in this case youth policy work. In order words, it is by looking ahead and sometimes basing upon past experiences that one can think about in terms of youth policy and what is the best legacy for this segment of the population. To this end, a section on the discussions of youth memories and expectations of the Games is presented by digging more profoundly into the participants' enactments of their recollections and imaginaries of these events as a valuable intangible legacy.

Although the portfolio that host cities normally need to put together in the bidding process comprises a detailed legacy plan, such documents are seen as mainly focusing on topics viewed as catalysts for different societal matters, such as the reduction of crime, increasing sports participation and sharing the values of the Olympic Movement (Coalter, 2004; Bullough, 2012), all perceived, arguably, as what Kohe and Collison (2019) designate as a normalised discourse of 'civic good'. This is often seen by some scholars as problematic and, to some extent, even contentious when it comes to the Olympic citizenship values focused on the younger population. A great deal of the criticism on the Olympic education and youth development is focused on the increasing participation of corporate partnerships with the Olympic entities, at the local and national levels, to make an impact on change and action on youth citizenship. The problem lies on the corporate interests with the IOC endorsement, in which sport–corporate–education nexus becomes part of the Olympics agenda and its legacy discourse, yet not necessarily benefiting the local communities or audiences in these particular contexts (Kohe & Collison, 2019; Wise & Kohe, 2020).

Yet, the same topics also relate, by and large, to how young people imagine and understand their societies within and beyond national contexts. In other words, in the case of young people, the idea around an Olympic legacy or legacies is often applied with a focus on sports participation (Chappelet, 2012; Veal et al., 2012; Kohe & Bowen-Jones, 2016) and the legacies in connection to the Olympic Movement (Girginov &

Hills, 2008; Thorpe & Wheaton, 2011). Without taking away its value, especially in relation to young citizens' understanding of sports and Olympic values, the idea of legacy is further explored in this book, but from a social and immaterial context, particularly in relation to cultural policy targeted at young people.

As a result, legacy or legacies are assessed and reviewed along the chapters of this book from an intangible and social phenomena perspective, and as a cross-examination of youth citizenship or civic engagement, somewhat similar to what Pierre de Coubertin[5] had idealised for the modern Olympics: more than just a sports event—a philosophy of life. Thus, the Games are framed beyond their contribution to youth physical development but also as an excellent platform for promoting values and fostering different identity performances (Donnelly & Young, 1988; Fraser-Thomas et al., 2005; Green, 2010) and allow for the inclusion of different views and participation in society, significant to youth identity and citizenship across different times and spaces.

The Olympics' Legacy and the Implications for Youth Policy

Considered an important part of the wider public sphere, young people are recurrently targeted in governmental policies and other important public initiatives (Bessant, 2003; Ekholm & Lindström Sol, 2020). An example of this is the creation of a Youth Olympic Games (YOG) by the IOC, which despite not being the focus of this study, it will be used and referred interchangeably with the Summer Olympic Games, given the importance to set out some of the arguments put forward in relation to the IOC aims and values for young people. The YOG were created by the IOC in 2007, with the aim of being the flagship strategy for young people (Wong, 2011). Accordingly, the YOC was set up with the view of offering a place specifically for young people where not only they could compete in similar lines as the IOC competitions but also it became possible for them to learn about 'sports, culture, and education relating to the Olympic

---

[5] Pierre de Coubertin, a French aristocrat, historian and educator, was known as the father of the modern Olympic Games. He founded the International Olympic Committee and served as its second President. Coubertin envisioned the modern Olympic Games as similar to Games held in ancient Greece and encouraged the multiple and diverse participation of athletes (Kwauk, 2008; MacAloon, 2008).

Values of Excellence, Friendship, and Respect' (IOC, 2016; Kinoshita et al., 2023). In addition, these ideals are claimed to go beyond the field of competition of play. They are seen as ideals that could be integrated in the daily lives of any young citizen, despite being or not an athlete. Hence, they may well comprise of a range of initiatives and activities for this group, such as Young Reports, YOG Ambassadors and Athlete Role Models, as part of the event's experience (Hanstad et al., 2013). It was only in 2010 that the YOG took off in Singapore as the first official Summer Youth Olympic Games. Similar to the Summer Olympic Games, the YOG also has its legacy plans, one of them being, for example, the intangible legacies around youth perceptions of the Games, Olympism values or even a sense of national pride triggered by the event (Seidl et al., 2021). The use of role models (Stålstrøm et al., 2023) is an example of how the YOG maximised on the ideals of the Olympic movement to pass such values to other generations. Yet, the idea of integrating young people as part of the Olympic Movement in a more competitive way, like through Youth Olympic Games is relatively new. There are various arguments supporting the rationale behind a Youth Olympic Games. Some claim that former IOC President Jacques Rogge always had this idea in mind as his personal plan, with the aim of setting up a competition for young people to promote youth sports at an Olympic level, almost an extension of the IOC. Other critiques view it as a need to fill a gap and strengthen the Olympic Movement both from the IOC and from the National Olympic Committee points of view, at a local level (Hanstad et al., 2013). Either way, there are no doubts that the creation of a Youth Olympic Games certainly benefited many young people, in particular young athletes, who had the opportunity to compete at a higher level. Yet, aside from sports, the Games were also designed to include young people in leading roles. The aims here were also to expand the objectives of the IOC Culture and Education Programme and promote the Olympic values amongst young people (Hanstad et al., 2013; Prüschenk & Kurscheidt, 2017; Wong, 2011).

Since the first YOG in Singapore, a great deal of research has been done with the focus on the legacies and impact of the YOG on the younger generation. A recent example of this is the work on the impact of *Transforma*—Rio de Janeiro's education programme—focused on educational legacies for the youth, which suggests that such legacies need some sort of continuation if they are meant to have an impact in the long term. This includes, as well, longitudinal research that can incorporate insights from children and young people before, during and after the event

(Kirakosyan, 2020). Yet, like the Summer Olympic and Paralympic Games, the Youth Olympic Games have not been spared of criticism (Thorpe, 2022; Staalstroem, 2021). For example, the idea of embracing young people from all walks of life and contexts in the Olympic Movement and sports participation is yet to be fulfilled. Accordingly, sports and human rights, particularly when it comes to Children Rights, go hand in hand in terms of criticism. The same applies to the view that the IOC aim with the YG is simply to keep TV audiences and rates up, by overlooking the so-claimed statement of tackling youth obesity (Wong, 2011, p. 1846; Zhou et al., 2020). The fact remains that since the introduction of the YOG, it is still debatable whether the Games have indeed been a contributor (or not) to reduce global obesity (Grayson, 2021). Another strategy put into place by the YOG was the Olympic Values Education Programme (OVEP), which was integrated into schools in order to address the following three components: (a) launch an educational reference manual, called Teaching Values; (b) create an interactive database for the exchange of actions and initiatives; (c) set up a label (created in 2009) with the view to encourage teachers, educators and others working in this field who have offered an education based on the Olympic values. Such programmes have at their root the IOC's values which in turn have been criticised for being rather simplistic and unspecific (Binder, 2012; Hsu & Kohe, 2015). In turn, the OVEPs are always inevitably dependent on the 'social, political, cultural, and educational contexts' where they are implemented (Hwang & Henry, 2023, p. 563).

Overall, when looking at the legacies of the YOG achieved so far, one aspect that comes up is the need to look beyond youth participation and add to that more research focused on sports through the community (ibid.). As such, part of the findings discussed in this book can be used to explore further young people's needs and views in relation to the Games, including sports participation and how they perceive some of the topics elevated by the YOG regarding the Olympic Movement. I was able to explore, in more detail, the importance of some sports in countries like Brazil and its relationship with class structure and access. The same applies to other countries where the Youth Olympic Games might have taken place or will be taking place in the near future. What I suggest, as way of conclusion, and based on the findings from this study, is that each case, be it local, or national, should be looked in isolation and by integrating young people in the decision making, when planning the Games.

More specifically, in the case of this study, the narrative from the Olympic organisations and the host cities throughout the bidding process for the London and Rio de Janeiro Games also reveals the importance of this public, where a particular type of rhetoric is used based on an emotional view of these young inhabitants as future citizens. The so-called 'youth question' is equally reinforced here as a complex topic that has nonetheless been under scrutiny by governments, policymakers and researchers, regarding their engagement with the public sphere (Cammaerts et al., 2014; Briggs, 2017). The idea of youth as targets of these government discourses is contested and problematised in this book, suggesting a rather 'youth-washing' approach known for being applied in other contexts with young people by governmental entities and NGOs, for example, for important causes (Gorman, 2021; Hawkins, 2024) with the caveat that is not produced with young people's best interests in mind (Loncle-Moriceau & Pickard, 2023). Instead, what is suggested is that, as part of such events' legacy plans and discourses, further consultation with or a closer examination of young people's views is required. The problem often relates to the view of young people as a homogenous group when, in fact, they are, as adults, active social actors with complex identities and their own lived experiences (Burke, 2005; Giugni & Grasso, 2021; Grassi et al., 2024; Weller, 2007; Tsekoura, 2016). This approach is critical to understanding the multiple views of young people including their own identities and to rethink the impact of the Olympic Games legacies in line with the youth policy agenda in each country where the Games take place. It also deconstructs the content of some of the discourses from governments and Olympic entities while using the youth as a strategy to achieve their aims, instead of addressing the concerns raised by some of the young citizens.

In order to contextualise and understand the work on youth policy developed alongside the Olympic Games, I draw attention to the specificities of the two case studies presented in this book in the respective cities of London and Rio de Janeiro. In particular, I look at the multiple concepts and considerations attached to youth citizenship, cultural policy and place-making in these settings and how they may influence, determine or shape the youth policy agenda of the Olympic Games.

Youth Citizenship in the United Kingdom

Given that one part of the fieldwork for this research was conducted in the United Kingdom during the 2012 Summer Olympic and Paralympic Games, it made sense to touch upon the key moments on the constructions of youth citizenship in this country by providing an overview on the development and critical periods associated with this concept. Contextualising notions of youth citizenship in the United Kingdom will help us to better understand some of the enactments and expressions from these people, despite their differences and diversity.

Overall, debates on youth citizenship in the United Kingdom, over the last two decades, have been largely polarised, which in turn makes it more difficult to set out a specific agenda for youth policy in light of mega-events. On the one hand, there has been a growing interest in what is perceived as a crisis based on young people's alienation and disengagement from politics and traditional formats of citizenship (Buckingham, 2000; Mycock & Tonge, 2011; Sakib, 2021; Sloam, 2011a, b). Policy-makers have been expressing a concern over what may be seen as a crisis of citizenship values in young people, not only in the United Kingdom but across other Western democratic societies. However, on the other hand, research on this topic has equally suggested that when young populations manifest themselves as active citizens, they more often do so by mobilising themselves politically outside the system (Swartz & Arnot, 2014; Beaunier & Veneti, 2020; Kitanova, 2020), which could translate into active engagement and participation on local causes or topics that are might not specifically be on the government's agenda, but still relevant for this group. This suggests that further attention should be paid to the fact that the apparent decline in youth engagement with traditional political participation could have been replaced, to some extent, by alternative forms of engagement outside the political system (Bessant, 2020; Boulianne & Theocharis, 2020; Cho et al., 2020; Marsh et al., 2007; Sloam, 2007, 2014). Another example of the importance of youth citizenship is the idea of empowerment and how youth policies might be developed in order to other less or marginalised groups to have their own space and voice as active citizens. To this end, the work of Claire Wallace (2018) focused on European citizenship is relevant to draw some parallels with part of this book's arguments in relation to how such mega-events may provide an opportunity to empower youth citizenship.

The 2011 riots that took place in the United Kingdom, and now more recently the counter-protests against right-wing, racism and xenophobia protests, are just some examples of this alternative form of engagement which, similar to other manifestations in Europe and the rest of the world, illustrate rather well this newly developed repertoire of civic and political engagement.[6]

Despite various initiatives from the UK government (e.g. introducing a Citizenship module in the English National Curriculum, and the establishment of the Youth Citizenship Commission—YCC), young people in the United Kingdom still appear to show more interest in the moral aspects of citizenship as opposed to the political aspects (Haste & Hogan, 2006). Also, the development of new technologies, such as online platforms, has created new webs of connections and enabled the dissemination of information globally which, along with its risks and opportunities, have opened up an array of new ways to mobilise and to encourage political engagement. In the case of world mega and sport events, there is evidence from previous cases that demonstrate how such events are used as a catalyst to debate and explore topics inherently linked to citizenship, such as human rights and other aspects of the interest of participants (Black & Bezanson, 2004; Stockdale, 2012). This explains, ultimately, why more bottom-up approaches to youth participation and civic engagement within society are necessary and potentially more efficient to meet young people's different needs (Sloam, 2007; Gerodimos, 2010; Paciello & Pioppi, 2014). Notions of belonging are therefore, in this context, shaped by social locations; identifications and emotional attachments; and ethical and political values (Swartz & Arnot, 2014, p. 6).

Despite the body of research on youth political engagement and citizenship in Britain, the development of young people's civic and political engagement has not been seen as explored in great detail (Nemcok & Wass, 2021; Sloam, 2011a, p. 1). Existing literature in this field often falls within the spectrum of what is considered traditional disengagement, on topics such as voting and participating directly in the political system. Hence, the dominant perspective fails to fully consider the alternative

---

[6] The 2011 riots in the United Kingdom, known as the London riots, were a series of riots taking place across the city of London between 6 and 11 August 2011. The protest started following the death of Mark Duggan who was shot by the police. For many, the riots were also symptomatic of a level of dissatisfaction amongst some people (mainly youngsters) from underprivileged and disadvantaged neighbourhoods with a high level of ethnic fractionalisation (Sloam, 2011a, b; Kawalerowicz & Biggs, 2015).

forms of citizenship, integrating emotional and cultural aspects, that some young inhabitants may develop in order to participate in and make sense of their society. What is argued is that the problem often lies in the fact that existing scholarship does explore in depth the potential of youth political imaginaries and expectations of their settings (Marsh et al., 2007, p. 4), which are also considered legitimate forms of citizenship. Also, in the case of the development of youth citizenship UK versus Europe, some scholars suggest that a new research agenda is necessary in order to address a gap in the literature in this area and provide a more intense and systematic interrogations of the meanings and developments of citizenship within the changes of social and political arenas for the youth (Bynner et al., 2019).

Some of the points identified here are critical for addressing the deficits in both youth citizenship and youth policy research in the United Kingdom, with particular regard to the examination of youth political imaginaries and their views or feelings of the Olympic Games. These aspects are not only significant but are a valid form of active participation in society that needs to be taken on board when contemplating and planning such mega-events.

It is only from the 1990s onwards that youth studies in the United Kingdom began to pave a new way for the role of cultural geographies of youth identities or performances of civic engagement and develop an interest in 'everyday discourses that regulate social interactions with the local as a site of multiple contestations in and against the global city' (Cohen & Ainley, 2010, p. 88). These works suggest that on the whole cultural geographies theories are key to make sense of young people's relationship with their local settings and therefore should be brought in line with theories of youth citizenship, education, and policy studies, including global events with the profile and aims such as the Olympics. In addition to that, there also seems to be in the United Kingdom a pressing need for new approaches beyond the economic or cultural perspectives (Cohen & Ainley, 2010; Smith et al., 2005; Furlong et al., 2011), which in turn allows more space for other programmes and initiatives focused on the younger population.

Another interesting fact in the context of youth citizenship in the United Kingdom is that unlike other European countries, youth subcultures have prevailed in this country as opposed to youth movements (Cohen & Ainley, 2010, p. 80). Cultural expressions such as 'teddy boys', 'judies', 'punk' and 'goth' unveil types of youth cultural manifestations that still represent a change in traditional political terms in the United

Kingdom. Moreover, gender, race, ethnicity and class are perceived as important topics within UK sociological traditions, initially led by the Birmingham School in the 1970s and 1980s. In this book, I challenge some of the debates that position young people in the United Kingdom as the same or as having similar experiences, across local, national and transnational contexts (Rattansi & Phoenix, 2005, p. 102). Instead, I contemplate diversity such as gender, race and class, amongst other elements, as key for youth inclusion and engagement with society, while addressing key topics on the Olympic Games. Yet, it is worth noting that in the lead up to London 2012, there have been some important initiatives and progress by the UK government with implications for youth citizenship. For example, the development of sport policies and youth community initiatives, as part of Sport England and Greater London Authorities, such as the Model City London, which was a project aimed at improving social integration through sports and empowering local people to change things in their communities.

Youth Citizenship in Brazil

A review on the state of the art about youth participation and youth policy work in Brazil points to a long historical context of deep inequality that is still visible today, particularly when talking about youth policy in the context of Brazil and the Olympic Games. Accordingly, there seem to be two types of childhood in this country—experienced by the rich and the poor—which inevitably are acted upon in distinct ways in Brazil (Butler, 2008, p. 301). This differentiation, in turn, reflects the way young people are perceived and researched in this country from a sociological and policy work perspective, let alone the policy work towards mega-events, like the Olympics.

The socio-economic and spatial background of youth has been instrumental when considering the differences and the rights of children in Brazil and while exploring the key outcomes and intangible legacies of events like the Olympic Games. Despite the introduction of the Children and Adolescent Stature (ECA) in 1990, current perceptions around the inequalities faced by young people prevail within the population, the judiciary and the media (Butler, 2008, p. 303). This ultimately also has implications on who benefits from the legacies of mega-events and other initiatives put forward by the government towards these sporting events.

Alternative forms of citizenship in Brazil appear to develop from the 1980s onwards in connection with social movements that claimed to be working towards the democratisation process, particularly in countries with past authoritarian regimes such as Brazil (Dagnino, 2005, p. 2). The rationale behind such social movements was to redefine citizenship through the cultural dimensions of the country. Hence, 'concerns with subjectivities, identities, and the right to difference' (ibid.) were at stake here. For example, Paulo Freire's Pedagogy of the Oppressed[7] was essential for supporting alternative ways of working with children and young people from less advantaged backgrounds.

For Udi Mandel Butler (2008), the development of youth citizenship in Brazil is intrinsically linked to three different interpretations and conceptualisations of youth. Accordingly, young people living in the favelas are often perceived by the Brazilian media and the middle class as a group at potential risk, prone to being recruited by drug trafficking gangs (Butler, 2008, 13 p. 306), which is problematic in terms of how one recalls or imagines the city and its young inhabitants in light of mega-events like the Olympics. Youth, in this case, are considered as a fragmented group needing to be treated according to their background and the types of risks they pose. Although youth is not a unitary category, from a sociological perspective, the fragmentation of this group as it happens in the case of Brazil is equally not beneficial for them.

Such assumptions have serious implications for youth citizenship research and the opportunities given to these young people to engage with society and the cultural events taking place in their settings. It also has implications when it comes to the work of policy makers and government entities in trying to embrace young people from all walks of life. Often what happens is that they fail to address young people's individual

---

[7] Popular Education was an approach to critical pedagogy introduced in many countries in the first half of the twentieth Century, with a strong tradition in Latin American countries. The concept implies a plethora of educational approaches focused mainly on the popular classes, working to serve their needs. It sought to challenge traditional formats of education, by using a dialectical or dialogic model between the teacher, the student and society. Paulo Freire was one of the most prominent figures of Brazil's Popular Education. His book *Pedagogy of the Oppressed* proposes a new approach to education. It critiques current traditional education pedagogies and instead suggests a new model where 'consciencializacao' is used as a way of understanding the world and taking action against oppressive elements in people's lives. Furthermore, Freire's work has been critiqued in various ways since it has been written by numerous authors. His pedagogy formed the basis of the development of participatory action research in the Latin American context (Borda, 2020).

needs and voices adequately by framing citizenship based on assumptions that disregard other forms of civic performances, such as alternative ones.

The second perspective put forward by Butler contemplates youth as a phase of experimentation whereby acts of citizenship result in different types of expressions and performances that impact on cultural forms and the arts (Butler, 2008, p. 307). These could include anything from music, the arts, theatre, cinema or video production, which all seem to be connected to methods of developing critical engagement and reflection. In such cases, the media involved in this process are critical to making young people's voices heard and prompting them to reflect on their social realities in relation to mass media representations of youth and the exclusion of marginalised communities (Butler, 2008, p. 307).

The last approach hinges on a utopian view of youth citizenship, whereby this group is seen as the hope in Brazil and subject of change for society, particularly in the case of Brazil, as manifested by movements such as the MST—Landless Movement. All these different approaches to youth citizenship in Brazil are useful to support and make sense of the findings discussed later on in this book, including the participants' diverse views on the Olympic Games. They also provide the rationale for informing new directions on youth policy regarding mega-events in the case of this country, which might be different from other settings.

Yet, the background of youth participation in Brazil is more diverse now than in the 1960s, for example, when it was composed mainly of middle-class young people (Abramo, 2005; Novaes, 2006). As a result, policy documents and approaches of Brazilian youth are increasingly more inclined to consider diversity at various levels, such as being connected to geography, and the new ways through which this group currently mobilises themselves in the wider public sphere and as part of their specific field of action or interest (Novaes, 2006, cited in Butler, 2008, p. 309).

CULTURAL POLICY AND PLACE-MAKING

Described as the 'set of social, political and material processes by which people interactively create and recreate the experienced geographies in which they live' (Pierce et al., 2011, p. 54), place-making is an important area of cultural policy relevant to citizenship studies and so equally important in the context of mega-events and the Olympic Games. Such events, like the Olympics, are claimed as bringing huge urban transformations to the cities where it takes place. Their legacies implicate changes in the images of the host cities, as part of spatial commodification that is inevitably maximised with the support of branding strategies, opening and closing ceremonies, amongst other aspects (Hanakata, 2022).

Cultural policy is intrinsically linked to the cultural industries, such as the media, the arts, and heritage, with implications at national, local, and transnational levels (Hesmondhalgh & Pratt, 2005). As part of governmental policies, cultural policy serves as a bridge between the arts, perceived in broad terms, and collective ways of life (Miller, 2010). It is, therefore, an important area to articulate the youth citizens' needs and desires around spaces, communities, arts, culture and other aspects of daily life. It also involves governmental strategies that seek to promote the marketing, dissemination and consumption of a plethora of activities related to culture. These can be anything from 'public support for museums',

> 'the visual arts, [...] the performing arts, [...] community celebrations, fairs and festivals' (ibid., p. 321). Cultural policy can often be applied to nation branding and as a soft power tool, particularly in the case of cultural events like the Olympics.' (de Almeida et al., 2014)

As a mass media and cultural event, the Olympic Games is a typical example of how a cultural phenomenon can be utilised as a promotional tool for the host city for the implementation of cultural policy strategies (Garcia, 2008, p. 362) beyond its role as a sporting competition. However, according to Garcia (2008), the Olympics offers both opportunities and challenges for policy-makers working in this field, especially when it covers different publics at the same time. As a cultural phenomenon, it has implications at local, national, transnational and mediated levels. In this book, I focus more specifically on the implications at a local level with the youth population. However, national or even transnational cultural policies already in place may also be relevant to the young participant's sense of belonging and engagement with the event. An example of this is the Olympic Cultural and Arts programming—the Cultural Olympiad—which supposedly was meant to played an instrumental role in the host cities' definition and development of cultural policies, despite recent criticism in relation to the lack of management and assessment of the projects implemented for the benefit of the wider public (Papanikolaou, 2013), including in this case the youth population. In fact, when it comes to the overall assessment of the London 2012 Cultural Olympiad programme, some of the frustrations and challenges identified by youth project managers and cultural institutions were, by and large, connected with the complexity of funding and partnership arrangements. From a management point of view, such problems limited the benefits of being part of the Olympic Games Cultural programme (Garcia, 2012, 2015).

The media, broadly speaking, have equally played a central role in this process, by portraying and disseminating the signs, rituals and images that are critical to the cultural staging of the Games (ibid., p. 361). This is why in this book I dedicate a chapter to explore the role of the media as a key player alongside policy work addressed at young people and in light of the Olympic Games.

Case Study 1. Contextualising Cultural Policy, Education and Place-Making in the United Kingdom

Cultural policy research in the United Kingdom evolved from the intersection of cultural studies, political theory, urban theory, sociology and cultural history, more recently including the role of cultural memory as an emerging and important field (Erll et al., 2008; Assmann, 2011).

The Birmingham School is an example that played a key role in influencing cultural policy in the United Kingdom. It was from the 1980s onwards that the term cultural policy shifted from a focus on high culture towards more inclusive forms of culture known as the cultural industries of broadcasting, film, popular music and fashion (Meredyth & Minson, 2000, p. xiii).

As future citizens and a specific group of society, young people have long been targeted in cultural policy documents in the United Kingdom (Bennett, 2003; Bessant, 2003; McGuigan, 2004; Ekholm & Lindström Sol, 2020). The same applies to education policy and other strategies that have capitalised on the opportunities of the Olympic Games as an event with a great potential to engage practitioners, the public and communities directly with sports education, government and the Olympic movement (Kohe & Chatziefstathiou, 2017). Legacy, in most of the cases such as the London 2012 Get Set programme, is by and large connected with the education-based programmes aimed at young people (Postlethwaite et al., 2020) but also contested for inevitably becoming part of the political and commercial aims of the host cities (Kohe & Collison, 2019).

Yet, there is still a paucity of studies around the cultural productivity of this group (Belfiore, 2020; Buckingham & Jones, 2001) which calls out for more research, both in terms of cultural policy as well as the education policy around the Olympic programmes set out by the host cities. This includes exploring the concept of Olympic Education, particularly around youth sports legacies, and the extent to which it provides the opportunity to prevent social exclusion, fostering bonding and bridging social capital among young people as a key legacy (Defroand, 2012). To this end, one aspect that is addressed in this book is the extent to which diversity and multiculturalism embedded in youths' lives might play an important role in how they negotiate ways of living, shared urban spaces and sites to engage in intercultural mixing (Butcher & Harris, 2010). In other words, I argue that little attention has been paid to how

> *the mundane realities of young people's everyday experiences of living with multiculturalism, where much larger questions of citizenship, national identity, belonging and community are worked over in quotidian ways.*
> (Butcher & Harris, 2010, p. 450)

Such approach includes contemplating the realities and diversity of young people in the educational programmes and legacies set out by the IOC and the host cities. In the case of London, specifically, the Get Set Programme was created as the official education programme of London 2012 Summer Olympic and Paralympic Games. The aim was to inspire and educate children aged between 3 and 19 years old all over the United Kingdom based on the Olympic values. This included excellence, friendship, respect, determination and inspiration, amongst other values. The programme reached out different schools across the United Kingdom with the aim of spreading the Olympic spirit and educate these young people about the Olympic values. Some critics point out that the aims of London 2012 education programme failed to meet young people in the area where the Games took place, in East End of London. Despite the fact that the programme was not compulsory but rather implemented at the heart of the schools with a plethora of resources for teachers to utilise, young people in East End who were arguably instrumental in the bid for the Games were left with a sense that those promises were never going to be fulfilled (Evans, 2016).

Studies focused on the Olympic Games' policies and education for young people, including the plans set out by the IOC and the Youth Olympic Games, suggest that this societal group is recurrently targeted in Games' discourse in light of the city aims and legacy for the youth population. This argument is often based on what the IOC already proclaims, which is with the view to inspiring young people around the world to engage in sports and ultimately adopt a life by the standards of the Olympic values (Hanstad et al., 2013). As a result, Olympic host cities, like in the case of London, are now required to organise and deliver an education programme as part of their bidding process and legacy plan. Yet, according to some scholars, there is little information on the impact and outcomes of schools' engagement with such programmes. Accordingly, most of the outcomes and assessment of these programmes are done by the governments instead of being examined by academics (Chen & Henry, 2020), leaving therefore an opportunity and gap to be addressed by researchers, like in the case of this study.

During the London 2012 Games, both former president of the London Organising Committee for the Summer Olympic Games (LOCOG), Sebastian Coe, and Shadow Olympics Minister Tessa Jowell's speeches at the 2012 Olympics addressed young people as an important element of the legacy, setting out a similar tone that suggested unity and, to say the least, somewhat declared youth to be a homogenised group. In this book, such idea is contested and, unlike Sebastian Coe speech below, I instead contemplate and explore the diverse experiences and meanings and from young people with regard to the Games and the city itself, including the expectations in relation to the education programmes:

> *Choose London today and you send a clear message to the youth of the world: more than ever, the Olympic Games are for you.* (Sebastian Coe, 6 July 2005, The Telegraph, 2009, n.p.)

Co-ordinated by the Department of Culture, Media and Sports (DCMS), now the Department of Digital, Culture, Media and Sports, London's official bidding discourse was heavily focused on young people and a legacy of hope and inspiration, underpinned by the idea of the Games as a stimulus for a positive change. This type of discourse, including various speeches by Lord Coe[8] was targeted at the younger generation by encouraging positive change within the youth population, calling for

---

[8] Lord Sebastian Coe was the Chairman of the LOCOG, who headed up the bid to host the Games in London.

He is also a British politician and former track and field athlete. As a middle-distance runner, Coe won four Olympic medals, including 1500 metres gold medals at the Olympic Games in 1980 and 1984.

better levels of participation in sports, and maximising the opportunities of Olympic values for future and better citizenship (Kohe, 2017). Such discourse is not different from what other Olympic host cities used, where part of their intangible legacies plans were framed mainly around physical education initiatives directed and young people within the realm of education policy. London 2012 Get Set Programme is an example that will be explored further in this book, given that a large part of the fieldwork took place in school contexts where some of the participants revealed to be involved in the education programme of the Olympic Games. Yet, there are other examples along the history of the Games where the same approach towards the idea of intangible legacy is visible. From Athens 2004 (Makris & Georgiadis, 2017), Brazil's *Transforma* programme (Kirakosyan, 2020), Tokyo's *Yoi Don* (Chiabaut, 2021) and more recently Paris education programme *Generation 2024* (Attali & Le Yondre, 2022), these are just some of the Games, to mention a few, where the education programmes were central to these cities' rhetoric in relation to the long-lasting legacy promises. The fact remains that the education programme has become a central part of the host cities, almost like a contractual obligation between the two, for the development of various educational initiatives with the aim of promoting the ideals of Olympism (Kohe et al., 2022). The impact of the Olympic education programmes across the spectrum of cultural and education policies is significant, given that it is through the Cultural and Education programme that the IOC claims that the Olympism is upheld. In other words, the concept and values underpinning Olympism blend these two aspects of the plans, education and culture.

In the case of London, at the final bid event, the proponents were 'allowed 100 representatives in the voting hall, and in a bold move, bid leaders made sure 30 of them were young people from the capital' (BBC, 2005, n.p.). 'Inspire a Generation' was therefore used as the key slogan to capitalise on the effect of a mega-event not only in sports but also across other areas such as health, culture and education. The effect of London 2012 education programme was such that other host cities after London 2012 Games also invested heavily in their education programmes. 'Inspire a Generation' was therefore seen as a pioneering educational programme involving different stakeholders and demonstrating a 'commitment to wider issues related to legacy, youth investment and national sport-physical activity policy' (Bloyce & Lovett, 2016; Bullough, 2012; Devine, 2017).

Despite efforts from the London Organising Committee of the Olympic and Paralympic Games (LOCOG), there is little evidence to support the long-lasting legacy promised for young people in London, with particular regards to the gift or social legacies (MacRury & Poynter, 2010). Research on this topic suggests quite the opposite of what was proposed in London, especially for the youth population of East London. Paul Watt (2013), for example, looks at how the regeneration in East London affected the overall positive idea of legacy of the London 2012 Games. Gentrification in this part of the city was heightened as a result of the Olympic Games (Watt, 2013, p. 114), which ultimately also impacted upon how people experienced their local settings in light of such events, including how they embraced the Games from a perspective of education and cultural policy approaches.

Furthermore, the changes brought by the Games were perceived by some as negative and a threat to young people's sense of place, which reveals an important finding for place-making and policy work in this sense. Displacement was also identified as taking place during the Games, particularly affecting the youth population in areas such as East London (Watt, 2013, p. 114).

One of the difficult tasks of policy makers is to ensure that events like the Olympic Games are maximised by balancing risks and opportunities. When the plan does not quite go according to plan, the pitfalls of social legacies are always exposed and, in the case of the Olympics, such plans are scrutinised like any other mega-event with such implications. It is for this reason that public consultation prior to the event is paramount, in particular regarding young people's views which also need to be taken into account as equally as those of other citizens while devising new policies. The question remains as to whether London 2012 Olympic Games' education programme and plans towards young people really inspired a generation. While some scholars point to a gap in research in this field, arguing that the London Inspire project has received little scholarly scrutiny (Girginov, 2016) others suggest that the programme and its agenda are somewhat enforced to physical education teachers and students, creating some pressure to inspire and engage young people in sport activities, when the reality in the long run is not the same as it is expected in terms of sport education legacy aims (Kohe & Bowen-Jones, 2016).

The fact remains that both the education and cultural programmes of the Olympic Games are viewed as instrumental for a successful bid, as they set up promises around intangible legacies related to the development of the spirit of Olympism. In fact, both the education and cultural policies of host cities are intrinsically related in this sense, as the values of Olympism are viewed as philosophy of life not just involving sports but also impacting upon the cultural lives in spreading and popularising the cultural aspects important for citizenry (Zhong et al., 2022).

To this end, and in parallel to the educational programme, the 2012 Olympic Games Cultural Programme, the Cultural Olympiad[9]—a compulsory cultural programme established by the IOC regulations and run in parallel with the Olympic Games—was introduced as a good opportunity to maximise the city's cultural policy and engage young people in different aspects of the Games. However, none of the regulations set out by the cultural programme clarified their exact function, which in turn led to: 'a gap between the eagerness of potential host cities to propose activities for the cultural Olympic programme at the bid stage and the readiness of the chosen Olympic organising committee to implement them' (Garcia, 2008, p. 373).

Funded by the Arts Council, Legacy Trust UK and the Olympic Lottery Distributed, the Cultural Olympiad of the London 2012 Olympic Games consisted of a specific programme of cultural events across the United Kingdom for four years (2008–2012). Young people, regeneration and the future were the fundamentals underpinning the 2012 Legacy plan (Scott, 2014, p. 8). Although the official documentation related to the London Cultural Olympiad for the 2012 Games does not specify in concrete what it is meant by young people, the subsequent reports identify an age bracket between 16 and 24, as the young citizens who were more engaged and motivated to take part in the cultural activities (Garcia & Cox, 2013). However, similar to previous Games in other cities, the success of the London Cultural Olympiad proved to be difficult to evaluate, given the variety and volume of programmes across the country (Kennell & MacLeod, 2009). Statistical outcomes rather than more complex qualitative evaluations (Scott, 2014) are often presented as key findings of the Games, whereas participation and social cohesion were overlooked by the Olympic Cultural programmes (Beauvais & Jenson, 2002; McCarthy, 2006). These aspects are viewed as significant in the field of cultural

---

[9] The Cultural Olympiad is a cultural programme part of the official Olympic event. It comprises different cultural events set up by the host country and with the view of involving different people from the country and outside, contributing to the respective cities' cultural policies (Garcia, 2008).

democracy, because they contemplate people's entitlement and access to culture (Hadley & Belfiore, 2018), which adds cultural value beyond economic perspectives and in relation to the education values of the Olympic Games.

The relationship identified between levels of participation and other social outcomes allows us to acknowledge other significant forms of participation and ideas of civic engagement (Scott, 2014, p. 14), both at the education and cultural levels. In particular, it categorises who is able to participate and who is included within or excluded from public debate and engagement with the city or nation and with events such as the Games with high impact on the cities. This book relies on theories such as the work of scholars like Belfiore (2020), who claim that cultural policy measures should move away from the economic doxa and instead include groups from different social contexts for the benefit of other cultural policy discourses. I argue the same for the education programmes of the Games. One intangible yet significant legacy of the Olympic Games explored in this book is its social legacy, which opens up other ways of exploring how opportunities for performances, displays and the exercise of 'civil society' (Roche, 2002, p. 13) are instigated. As an integral part of the public sphere, young participants' voices, views, stories and civic enactments, underpinned by their memories and expectations of the Games are key to making sense of the legacy outcomes and to better understanding what citizenship means to them (Kohe, 2017). It is precisely around the memories of London 2012 Games that this book seeks to contribute to a better understanding of the legacies of the Games, which includes as well enactments of active citizenship.

Case Study 2. Cultural Policy, Education and Place-Making in Brazil

The development of education and cultural policies in Brazil has always been historically linked to questions of human rights, democratisation, identity and enactments of citizenship (Moreira & Calabre, 2012). As a result, the idea of citizenship and education or culture are, one way or the other, two aspects that have long been interwoven and thus relevant for making sense of Brazilian cultural policies, especially when looking at the policies set out by mega-events taking place in the country.

It was not until 1988, following the promulgation of the Constitution of Brazil, that bottom-up revindications and civil mobilisations began to emerge, underpinned by the development of cultural policies (Moreira &

Calabre, 2012). Described as a 'decade of reforms', the 1990s were a significant period for Brazil and a 'turning point in the economic history of the country' (Baumann, 2002, p. 6), particularly for culture policy. During this decade, nearly 21% of Brazil's GDP was allocated to public social programmes, including areas related to education and culture as a move to channel spending into the social sphere (Baumann, 2002, p. 92). Although the Lei Rouanet (in English Rouanet Law), was an important milestone for the cultural sector in Brazil, it was later criticised for leaving too much power and public resources in the hands of a few wealthy business people in Brazil. Criticisms directed at this policy were substantiated on the basis of the following idea:

> *Culture became a prime victim of globalisation; the commodification of the world invading the cultural sphere in devastating fashion. From infinite diversity, Brazilian culture was reduced to the clichés of soap operas. Brazil was reconstructed in the national imagination by television. Cultural representation dwindled to three or four chic districts of São Paulo and Rio de Janeiro, with a few scenes from the country's folklore thrown in (for export). The absence of the rich diversity of Brazilian people in the nation's history and imagination was thus consolidated.* (Turino, 2018, p. 24)

All these trajectories of Brazil's cultural policies are relevant to contextualise and set out the scene in relation to the 2016 Olympic Games in Rio de Janeiro and its impact on the youth population. Specially regarding the existing challenges and fights to overcome authoritarian and elitist approaches to culture and also to better understand the instrumentalisation of culture and education as key in this process.

The historical relationship between authoritarianism education and culture is not restricted to the dictatorship period in Brazil (Rubim, 2013). In fact, authoritarianism still prevails in the Brazilian society, and it is rooted in social inequalities, suggesting that elitism is 'expressed, at a macro-social level, through ignorance, persecution and annihilation of cultures including the cultural exclusion to which a significant part of the population is subject' (Rubim, 2013, pp. 246–247). This also includes inequality in terms of the educational and cultural access of minority groups, indigenous and African-Brazilian descendants, to media cultures, all of which are key when assessing the outcomes and history of legacies of the mega-events, given that these groups are 'hardly covered by the national cultural policies when they existed' (ibid., p. 247).

A new era of cultural policies developed by ministers Gilberto Gil and Juca Ferreira during President Lula's mandate (2002–2010) challenged this pattern and paved the way for the state's active role in different cultural and educational areas. The idea of society as the main producers and creators of culture is an important perspective of bottom-up approaches to culture, which seek to work towards 'opening paths to face authoritarianism' (Rubim, 2013, p. 251). Existing literature suggests that such policies, stemming from the National Cultural Plan (NCP) and National Cultural System (NCS), proved to be very popular and successful across the country especially for young people from deprived and less privileged backgrounds in Brazil (Vilutis, 2011, p. 111). As a result, a new multicultural approach to culture developed into multiple local projects that sought to challenge bureaucratic and traditional formats established in previous policies. Such new approach also gave more visibility to other forms of cultural expressions like the Cultura Viva - Pontos de Cultura (Points of Culture), which brought into being, 'points, places, and practices of cultures where the people have been "de-silenced"' (Turino, 2018, p. 24). In a nutshell, Pontos de Cultura enabled multiple voices from different parts of Brazil to find voice in a variety of arts and cultural expressions as well as learn further about their own culture. This included anything from music to literature, poetry and other popular artistic enactments. The cultural policies developed during Gil's mandate gave currency to that 'imperfect mosaic' of Brazilian culture (ibid., p. 13) in a fashion that had, arguably, never been explored before, and which is still very useful to embrace diversity in cultural policies. This book focuses on this idea of policy by adding as well the contribution of educational policies in light of the Games, defined as a way to 'perform a kind of anthropological acupuncture, massaging meridians and spaces which have become temporarily unvalued or dormant in the cultural body of the nation' (ibid., pp. 99–100) in order to establish connections with participants' memories and imaginaries and their multicultural contributions to cultural policy. I believe that this approach allows us to examine the benefits presented to young people from different walks of life who are able to voice their views of society, create new cultural spaces, and exercise the right to access culture and education. Most importantly, aspects of inclusion are equally foregrounded in such policy, which is critical for democracy and citizenship, and of the interest of this study.

According to Vilutis (2011, p. 115), young people's participation in such cultural and educational activities is viewed as promoting local citizenship, and engagement in politics and allows them to explore different constructions of identities, which is beneficial for them and for those working on youth policies.

Although it was during Lula's mandate that Rio de Janeiro made its formal bid for the 2016 Olympic Games (in 2009), the above-mentioned cultural policies and the promise to develop youth education programmes to promote the Olympic values as a commitment from the organisers (Kirakosyan, 2020) were regretfully never fully implemented. In fact, what is argued by many scholars in relation to the education plans is that like London, in Brazil the education programme *Transforma* lacked a critical pedagogical approach to frame its materials and was therefore discontinued after the Games were over (dos Santos, 2018). Also, Rio de Janeiro's local culture was largely overlooked (Calabre et al., 2017) because of the economic and political crisis that took over the country ahead of the Games (e.g. President Dilma's imminent impeachment and other political resignations). Instead, Rio de Janeiro opted to put forward a cultural plan to sell itself as a creative city (Florida, 2005; Szaniecki & Silva, 2010; Landry, 2012), by showcasing the best of the nation, with a cultural policy focused mainly on the production and consumption aspects of the city and the country to the outside world. As a result, the creative industry side of the Olympic Games prospered over the local culture. Rio de Janeiro's Cultural Olympiad[10]—the official Olympic Cultural Programme—was also relevant to the city's and Brazil's cultural policies. Rio de Janeiro was the first South American city to host the Summer Olympic and Paralympic Games, and as a result, it did not have a four-year Olympiad programme similar to all previous host cities. Instead, the programme was devised on the basis of a series of short programmes that took place during the Games in 2016 (Garcia, 2016). Hence, the cultural side of the Games was organised by the Secretary of Tourism of the Rio Municipality (Olympic Boulevard programme) and the International Olympic Committee Foundation for Culture and Olympic Heritage. Under these circumstances, the absence of a Cultural Olympiad, with specific aims set out by the host city was criticised for making the cultural policies of the 2016 Games difficult to assess. As it turned out, 'visitors and residents remain largely unaware of the points of connection between a range of cultural

[10] Rio de Janeiro's Cultural Olympiad was named as *Celebra* and planned based on Brazil's varied culture. The Head of the Programme, Carla Camurati, stated that the cultural programme involved 'a comprehensive record of Brazilian culture, not just those that exist today but a broader tribute to Brazilian culture'.

expressions inspired by the Olympic Games' (Garcia, 2016, n.p.). Supported by three levels of government (federal, state and municipality), the discourse of Rio 2016 official bid focused on the 'celebration and transformation of the city' of Rio de Janeiro (IOC, 2016, p. 46). It claimed that it sought to include strategies aimed at increasing youth participation, social transformation through sport, regional sports leadership, global promotion and success (Silva & Cerdan, 2014, p. 99). Yet little is known on the consultation process with young people in relation to these programmes and plans. As a result, there is also scarce information to date regarding Rio 2016's intangible legacies, particularly from the perspective of the local population (Reis et al., 2014). Public consultation and participation are two aspects that are fundamental for a sustainable cultural policy (Pratt, 2005; Andrews, 2006; McCarthy, 2006), but in the case of Rio de Janeiro's Olympic Games, they both seemed to have been overlooked, as we will be able to see from the participants' discourse.

In these next chapters, I explore the steps taken in the fieldwork and subsequently provide a discussion on the main findings.

BIBLIOGRAPHY

Abramo, H. W. (2005). Condição juvenil no Brasil contemporâneo. *Retratos da Juventude Brasileira: Análises de Uma Pesquisa Nacional, 2*, 37–72.

Agha, N., Fairley, S., & Gibson, H. (2012). Considering legacy as a multidimensional construct: The legacy of the Olympic Games. *Sport Management Review, 15*(1), 125–139.

Andrews, C. J. (2006). Chap. 12: Rationality in policy decision making. In *Handbook of public policy analysis* (p. 161).

Arendt, H. (1958). *The human condition*. University of Chicago Press.

Assmann, J. (2011). Communicative and cultural memory. In P. Meusburger, M. Heffernan, & E. Wunder (Eds.), *Cultural memories. Knowledge and space* (pp. 15–27). Springer.

Assmann, J., & Czaplicka, J. (1995). Collective memory and cultural identity. *New German Critique, 65*, 125–133.

Attali, M., & Le Yondre, F. (2022). Olympic education in France: A legacy issue or the promotion of a model in crisis? *Social Sciences, 11*(2), 62.

Baumann, R. (2002). Brazil in the 1990s: An economy in transition. In *Brazil in the 1990s: An economy in transition* (pp. 1–38). Palgrave/St. Antony's College.

Beaunier, J., & Veneti, A. (2020). Social media and political participation among British youth. *Journal of Promotional Communications, 8*(1).

Beauvais, C., & Jenson, J. (2002). *Social cohesion: Updating the state of the research* (Vol. 62). CPRN.

Belfiore, E. (2020). Whose cultural value? Representation, power and creative industries. *International Journal of Cultural Policy, 26*(3), 383–397.

Bennett, W. (2003). Communicating global activism. *Information, Communication & Society, 6*(2), 143–168.

Bessant, J. (2003). Youth participation: A new mode of government. *Policy Studies, 24*(2–3), 87–100. https://doi.org/10.1080/0144287032000170984

Bessant, J. (2020). *Making-up people: Youth, truth and politics.* Routledge.

Bessant, J., Collin, P., & Watts, R. (2024). A revisionist account of the crisis of democracy and 'youth participation'. In *Research handbook on the sociology of youth* (pp. 23–38). Edward Elgar Publishing.

Binder, D. L. (2012). Olympic values education: Evolution of a pedagogy. *Educational Review, 64*(3), 275–302.

Black, D., & Bezanson, S. (2004). The Olympic Games, human rights and democratisation: Lessons from Seoul and implications for Beijing. *Third World Quarterly, 25*(7), 1245–1261.

Bloyce, D., & Lovett, E. (2016). Planning for the London 2012 Olympic and Paralympic legacy: A figurational analysis. In *The 'Olympic and Paralympic' effect on public policy* (pp. 61–78). Routledge.

Booth, D. (2024). Bidding for the Olympic Games: An anatomy of arguments. *Journal of Olympic Studies, 5*(1), 69–94.

Borda, O. F. (2020). Experiências teórico-práticas. *Cadernos CIMEAC, 10*(3), 192–248.

Borges Tavares, S. (2022). *Jovencivic: (Re) framing youth citizenship through memories and imaginaries of the Olympic Games* (London 2012 and Rio de Janeiro 2016) (Doctoral dissertation, King's College London).

Boulianne, S., & Theocharis, Y. (2020). Young people, digital media, and engagement: A meta-analysis of research. *Social Science Computer Review, 38*(2), 111–127.

Bourbillères, H., Gasparini, W., & Koebel, M. (2023). Local protests against the 2024 Olympic Games in European cities: The cases of the Rome, Hamburg, Budapest and Paris 2024 bids. *Sport in Society, 26*(1), 1–26.

Breeze, B. (2009). *Natural philanthropists: Findings of the family business philanthropy and social responsibility inquiry.* Institute for Family Business (UK).

Briggs, J. (2017). Young people and participation in Europe. In *Young people and political participation* (pp. 63–86). Palgrave Macmillan.

Brown, A. D., Gutman, Y., Freeman, L., Sodaro, A., & Coman, A. (2009). Introduction: Is an interdisciplinary field of memory studies possible? *International Journal of Politics, Culture, and Society IJPS, 22*, 117–124.

Buckingham, D. (2000). *The making of citizens: Young people, news, and politics.* Routledge.

Buckingham, D., & Jones, K. (2001). New labour's cultural turn: Some tensions in contemporary educational and cultural policy. *Journal of Education Policy, 16*(1), 1–14. https://doi.org/10.1080/02680930010009796

Budiasa, M. (2024). Communication politics in sports events (politicization or political sports event). *Pena Justisia: Media Komunikasi dan Kajian Hukum, 23*(2), 461–471.

Bullon-Cassis, L. (2024). "A game show at the end of the world" The currency of youth in UN climate summitry. *Journal of Youth Studies*, 1–18.

Bullough, S. J. (2012). A new look at the latent demand for sport and its potential to deliver a positive legacy for London 2012. *International Journal of Sport Policy and Politics, 4*(1), 39–54.

Burke, T. (2005). Postscript on citizenship. In *Youth policy and social inclusion: Critical debates with young people* (pp. 51–53).

Butcher, M., & Harris, A. (2010). Pedestrian crossings: Young people and everyday multiculturalism. *Journal of Intercultural Studies, 31*(5), 449–453. https://doi.org/10.1080/07256868.2010.513080

Butler, U. M. (2008). Children's participation in Brazil–A brief genealogy and recent innovations. *The International Journal of Children's Rights, 16*(3), 301–312.

Bynner, J., Chisholm, L., & Furlong, A. (2019). A new agenda for youth research. In *Youth, citizenship and social change in a European context* (pp. 3–14). Routledge.

Calabre, C., Cabral, E., & Siqueira, M. (2017). *Memoria das Olímpiadas no Brasil: Diálogos e Olhares, 2*. Fundação Casa Rio Barbosa.

Cammaerts, B., Bruter, M., Banaji, S., Harrison, S., & Anstead, N. (2014). The myth of youth apathy: Young Europeans' critical attitudes toward democratic life. *American Behavioral Scientist, 58*(5), 645–664.

Cashman, R. (1998, October). Olympic Legacy in an Olympic City: Monuments, museums and memory. In *Fourth International Symposium for Olympic Research; Global and Cultural Critique: Problematizing the Olympic Games* (pp. 107–114).

Chappelet, J. L. (2012). Mega sporting event legacy: A multifaceted concept. *Papeles de Europa, 25*, 76–86.

Chatziefstathiou, D. (2012). Active citizens and public policy: The example of the London 2012 Olympic Games. *International Journal of Sport Management, Recreation and Tourism, 9*, 23–33.

Chen, S., & Henry, I. (2020). Assessing Olympic legacy claims: Evaluating explanations of causal mechanisms and policy outcomes. *Evaluation, 26*(3), 275–295.

Chen, Y., Jin, G. Z., Kumar, N., & Shi, G. (2013). The promise of Beijing: Evaluating the impact of the 2008 Olympic Games on air quality. *Journal of Environmental Economics and Management, 66*(3), 424–443.

Chiabaut, I. (2021). Tokyo 2020 official mascots and their contribution to the promotion of Japan's culture and legacy. *Diagoras: International Academic Journal on Olympic Studies, 5*, 88–100.

Cho, A., Byrne, J., & Pelter, Z. (2020). Digital civic engagement by young people. *UNICEF Office of Global Insight and Policy*.

Coalter, F. (2004). *London 2012: A sustainable sporting legacy. After the Goldrush: A sustainable Olympics for London.* IPPR and Demos.

Cohen, P., & Ainley, P. (2010). In the country of the blind?: Youth studies and cultural studies in Britain. *Journal of Youth Studies, 3*(1), 79–95. https://doi.org/10.1080/136762600113059

Dagnino, E. (2005). Citizenship and the social in contemporary Brazil. In *After Neo-liberalism.*

Dayan, D., & Katz, E. (1994). *Media events: The life broadcasting of history.* Harvard University Press.

De Almeida, P. (2014). *Cultural and creative industries in europe: The where, the why and the how.* Research Papers on knowledge, innovation and enterprise.

Defroand, J. (2012). *London 2012: Olympic 'legacy', Olympic education and the development of social capital in physical education and school sport: A case study* (Doctoral dissertation, University of Birmingham).

Devine, C. (2017). London 2012 Olympic legacy: A big sporting society? In *Understanding UK sport policy in context* (pp. 95–117). Routledge.

Donnelly, P., & Young, K. (1988). The construction and confirmation of identity in sport subcultures. *Sociology of Sport Journal, 5*(3), 223–240.

dos Santos, A. L. P. (2018). The educational program of the Olympic Games—Rio 2016. *The International Journal of Sport and Society, 9*(2), 19.

Doustaly, C., & Zembri-Mary, G. (2024). Is urban planning returning to the past in search of a sustainable future? Exploring the six Paris and London Olympic Games (1900–2024). *Planning Perspectives, 39*(3), 675–700.

Ekholm, D., & Lindström Sol, S. (2020). Mobilising non-participant youth: Using sport and culture in local government policy to target social exclusion. *International Journal of Cultural Policy, 26*(4), 510–523.

Erll, A., Nünning, A., Erll, A., & Nünning, A. (Eds.). (2008). *Cultural memory studies: An international and interdisciplinary handbook.* Walter de Gruyter.

Evans, G. (2016). *London's Olympic legacy.* Palgrave Macmillan.

Florida, R. (2005). *Cities and the creative class.* Routledge.

Fraser-Thomas, J. L., Côté, J., & Deakin, J. (2005). Youth sport programs: An avenue to foster positive youth development. *Physical Education & Sport Pedagogy, 10*(1), 19–40.

Furlong, A., Woodman, D., & Wyn, J. (2011). Changing times, changing perspectives: Reconciling 'transition' and 'cultural' perspectives on youth and young adulthood. *Journal of Sociology, 47*(4), 355–370.

Garcia, B. (2008). One hundred years of cultural programming within the Olympic Games (1912–2012): Origins, evolution and projections. *International Journal of Cultural Policy, 14*(4), 361–376.

Garcia, B. (2012). *The Olympic Games and cultural policy.* Routledge.

Garcia, B. (2015). *Placing culture at the heart of the games: Achievements and challenges within the London 2012 Cultural Olympiad* (pp. 225–269). Routledge.

Garcia, B. (2016). *The Olympic Games varied layers of Cultural Programming.* [Blog] Research Beyond Borders. Retrieved September 20, 2019, from https://researchbeyondborders.wordpress.com/2016/08/19/the-olympic-games-varied-layers-of-cultural-programming/

Garcia, B., & Cox, T. (2013). *London 2012 cultural Olympiad evaluation.* Institute of Cultural Capital.

Garde-Hansen, J. (2011). *Media and memory.* Edinburgh University Press.

Gerodimos, R. (2010). *New media, new citizens: The terms and conditions of online youth civic engagement* (Doctoral dissertation, Bournemouth University).

Girginov, V. (2016). Has the London 2012 Olympic Inspire programme inspired a generation? A realist view. *European Physical Education Review, 22*(4), 490–505.

Girginov, V. (2018). *Rethinking Olympic legacy.* Routledge.

Girginov, V., & Hills, L. (2008). A sustainable sports legacy: Creating a link between the London Olympics and sports participation. *The International Journal of the History of Sport, 25*(14), 2091–2116.

Girginov, V., & Preuss, H. (2021). Towards a conceptual definition of intangible Olympic legacy. *International Journal of Event and Festival Management, 13*, 1–17.

Giugni, M., & Grasso, M. (2021). *Youth and politics in times of increasing inequalities* (pp. 1–26). Springer International Publishing.

Gorman, J. (2021). *Disobedient youth: Lessons from the youth climate strike movement.* Council of Europe.

Grassi, E. F. G., Portos, M., & Felicetti, A. (2024). Young people's attitudes towards democracy and political participation: Evidence from a cross-European study. *Government and Opposition, 59*(2), 582–604.

Gratton, C., Preuss, H., & Liu, D. (2015). *Economic legacy to cities from hosting mega sports events: a case study of Beijing 2008.* In *Routledge handbook of sport and legacy* (pp. 46–58). Routledge.

Grayson, S. (2021). Ten years on: The Youth Olympic Games (Yog) through the eyes of Australian athletes. *Diagoras: International Academic Journal on Olympic Studies, 5*, 43–57.

Green, K. (2010). *Key themes in youth sport.* Routledge.

Habermas, J. (1991). *The structural transformation of the public sphere: An inquiry into a category of bourgeois society.* MIT Press.

Hadley, S., & Belfiore, E. (2018). Cultural democracy and cultural policy. *Cultural Trends, 27*(3), 218–223. https://doi.org/10.1080/09548963.2018.1474009

Halbwachs, M. (1950 [1980]). *The collective memory.* Harper and Row.

Halbwachs, M. (1992). *On collective memory.* University of Chicago Press.

Hanakata, N. C. (2022). A critical review of urban mega interventions as trendsetters of urban development practice. In *Mega events, urban transformations and social citizenship* (pp. 67–79).

Hanstad, D. V., Parent, M. M., & Kristiansen, E. (2013). The Youth Olympic Games: The best of the Olympics or a poor copy? *European Sport Management Quarterly, 13*(3), 315–338.

Haste, H., & Hogan, A. (2006). Beyond conventional civic participation, beyond the moral-political divide: Young people and contemporary debates about citizenship. *Journal of Moral Education, 35*(4), 473–493.

Hawkins, J. (2024). *"Like greenwashing but for gender" A thematic analysis on how young women experience gendered practices and structures at the COP conferences.*

Hesmondhalgh, D., & Pratt, A. C. (2005). Cultural industries and cultural policy. *International Journal of Cultural Policy, 11*(1), 1–13. https://doi.org/10.1080/10286630500067598

Hoskins, A. (2001). New memory: Mediating history. *Historical Journal of Film Radio and Television, 21*(4), 333–346. https://doi.org/10.1080/01439680120075473

Hsu, L. H. L., & Kohe, G. Z. (2015). Aligning Olympic education with the Liberal Arts: A curriculum blueprint from Taiwan. *Physical Education and Sport Pedagogy, 20*(5), 474–489.

Hwang, B., & Henry, I. (2023). Identifying the field of Olympic education: A meta-narrative review. *European Sport Management Quarterly, 23*(2), 561–585.

IOC. (2016). *Report of the IOC Evaluation Committee.* Retrieved November 25, 2021, from https://stillmed.olympic.org/media/Document%20Library/OlympicOrg/Documents/Host-City-Elections/XXXI-Olympiad-2016/Report-of-the-IOC-Evaluation-Commission-for-the-Games-of-the-XXXI-Olympiad-in 2016.pdf

Kaplanidou, K., & Karadakis, K. (2010). Understanding the legacies of a host Olympic city: The case of the 2010 Vancouver Olympic Games. *Sport Marketing Quarterly, 19*(2), 110.

Karadakis, K., & Kaplanidou, K. (2012). Legacy perceptions among host and non-host Olympic Games residents: A longitudinal study of the 2010 Vancouver Olympic Games. *European Sport Management Quarterly, 12*, 243–264.

Kawalerowicz, J., & Biggs, M. (2015). Anarchy in the UK: Economic deprivation, social disorganization, and political grievances in the London Riot of 2011. *Social Forces, 94*(2), 673–698.

Kazmierski-Davie, G., & Ballouli, K. (2024). Identity dynamics in collegiate Olympic Athletes Post-Tokyo 2020: A pre-post study. *Journal of Intercollegiate Sport, 17*(1).

Keightley, E., & Pickering, M. (2012). The mnemonic imagination. In *The mnemonic imagination* (pp. 43–80). Palgrave Macmillan.

Kennell, J., & MacLeod, N. (2009). A grey literature review of the Cultural Olympiad. *Cultural Trends, 18*(1), 83–88.

Keogh, F., & Fraser, A. (2005). Why London won the Olympics. *BBC.* http://news.bbc.co.uk/sport2/hi/other_sports/olympics_2012/4618507.stm

Kinoshita, K., MacIntosh, E., & Parent, M. (2023). Social outcomes from participating in the Youth Olympic Games: The role of the service environment.
European Sport Management Quarterly, 23(2), 488–507.

Kirakosyan, L. (2020). Educational legacy of the Rio 2016 Games: Lessons for
youth engagement. *Societies, 10*(2), 39.

Kitanova, M. (2020). Youth political participation in the EU: Evidence from a
cross-national analysis. *Journal of Youth Studies, 23*(7), 819–836.

Kohe, G. Z. (2017). London 2012 (Re) calling: Youth memories and Olympic
'legacy' ether in the hinterland. *International Review for the Sociology of Sport,
52*(1), 24–44.

Kohe, G. Z., & Bowen-Jones, W. (2016). Rhetoric and realities of London 2012
Olympic education and participation 'legacies': Voices from the core and
periphery. *Sport, Education and Society, 21*(8), 1213–1229.

Kohe, G. Z., & Chatziefstathiou, D. (2017). London 2012: Olympic education in
the United Kingdom: Rethinking London 2012, learning 'legacies' and their
pedagogical potential. In *Olympic education* (pp. 60–72). Routledge.

Kohe, G. Z., & Collison, H. (2019). *Sport, education and corporatisation: Spaces
of connection, contestation and creativity.* Routledge.

Kohe, G. Z., Aramaki, A., Sekine, M., Masumoto, N., & Hsu, L. (2022).
Conceptualising L'Space Olympique: Tokyo 2020 Olympic education in
thought, production and action. *Educational Review, 74*(6), 1172–1198.

Kwauk, C. (2008). An Olympic education: From athletic colonization to international harmony. *Pathways: Critiques and Discourse in Olympic Research,* 523–533.

Landry, C. (2012). *The creative city: A toolkit for urban innovators.* Routledge.

Landsberg, A. (2004). *Prosthetic memory: The transformation of American remembrance in the age of mass culture.* Columbia University Press.

Lenskyj, H. J. (2008). *Olympic industry resistance: Challenging Olympic power and
propaganda.* State University of New York Press.

Livingstone, S., & Bober, M. (2005). *UK children go online.* London.

Loncle-Moriceau, P., & Pickard, S. (2023). Young people's political discourse:
Voice, efficacy and impact. In *The Routledge handbook of language and youth
culture* (pp. 379–391). Routledge.

MacAloon, J. J. (2008). 'Legacy' as managerial/magical discourse in contemporary Olympic affairs. *The International Journal of the History of Sport, 25*(14),
2060–2071.

MacRury, I., & Poynter, G. (2010). 'Team GB' and London 2012: The paradox
of national and global identities. *The International Journal of the History of
Sport, 27*(16–18), 2958–2975.

Makris, A., & Georgiadis, K. (2017). Athens 2004: Olympic education in Greece
during the Athens 2004 Olympic Games. In *Olympic education* (pp. 47–59).
Routledge.

Marsh, D., O'Toole, T., & Jones, S. (2007). *Young people and politics in the UK: Apathy or alienation?* Palgrave Macmillan.

McCarthy, J. (2006). Regeneration of cultural quarters: Public art for place image or place identity? *Journal of Urban Design, 11*(2), 243–262.

McGuigan, J. (2004). *Rethinking cultural policy.* Open University.

McGuinness, M. (2015). A critical examination of the London 2012 legacy. In *The impact of the 2012 Olympic and Paralympic Games: Diminishing contrasts, increasing varieties* (pp. 72–93). Palgrave Macmillan UK.

Meredyth, D., & Minson, J. (2000). Resourcing citizenries. *American Behavioral Scientist, 43*(9), 1374–1394.

Miller, T. (2010). Cultural policy. *The Encyclopedia of Literary and Cultural Theory.*

Misener, L., & Mason, D. S. (2006). Developing local citizenship through sporting events: Balancing community involvement and tourism development. *Current Issues in Tourism, 9*(4–5), 384–398.

Misener, L., Darcy, S., Legg, D., & Gilbert, K. (2013). Beyond Olympic legacy: Understanding Paralympic legacy through a thematic analysis. *Journal of Sport Management, 27*(4), 329–341. https://doi.org/10.1123/jsm.27.4.329

Monnin, È. (2021, September). Olympic Education and Host City of the Olympic Games: The example of Paris 2024. In *Olympic Education—History, theory, practice* (pp. 121–131). Meyer & Meyer Verlag.

Moreira, R., & Calabre, L. (2012). Financiamento da Cultura sob a ótica dos direitos culturais: Possibilidades e desafios do Plano Nacional de Cultura. *Políticas Culturais em Revista, 5*(2), 97–114.

Mycock, A., & Tonge, J. (2011). The party politics of youth citizenship and democratic engagement. *Parliamentary Affairs, 65*(1), 138–161.

Nemcok, M., & Wass, H. (2021). Generations and political engagement. In *Oxford research encyclopedia of politics.* Oxford University Press.

Nordhagen, S. E. (2021). Leveraging sporting events to create sport participation: A case study of the 2016 Youth Olympic Games. *International Journal of Sport Policy and Politics, 13*(3), 409–424.

Novaes, R. (2006). Os jovens de hoje: Contextos, diferenças e trajetórias. In *Culturas jovens: Novos mapas do afeto* (pp. 105–120). Jorge Zahar.

Orsini, A. (2022). Youth goals? Youth agency and the sustainable development goals. *Youth and Globalization, 4*(1), 108–139.

Owen, S., & Chambers, D. (2024). Volunteers' sense of (dis) connection at a sport event. *Leisure Sciences, 46*(2), 105–122.

Paciello, M. C., & Pioppi, D. (2014). *A comprehensive approach to the understanding of the dynamics of youth exclusion/inclusion and the prospects for youth-led change in the South and East Mediterranean* (No. 1, pp. 2–26). Working paper.

Papanikolaou, P. (2013). Athens 2004. Ten years later the Olympic infrastructure, the cultural Olympiad and the 'white elephant' syndrome. *Journal of Power, Politics and Governance, 1*(1), 1–9.

Papanikos, G. T. (2020). The participation legacy at Olympic Games. *Athens Journal of Sports, 7*(4), 251–262.

Pfister, G. (2013). Lieux de mémoire/sites of memories and the Olympic Games: An introduction. In *Sport, memory and nationhood in Japan* (pp. 10–27). Routledge.

Pierce, J., Martin, D. G., & Murphy, J. T. (2011). Relational place-making: The networked politics of place. *Transactions of the Institute of British Geographers, 36*(1), 54–70.

Postlethwaite, V., Kohe, G. Z., & Molnar, G. (2020). Inspiring a generation: An examination of stakeholder relations in the context of London 2012 Olympics and Paralympics educational programmes. In *Creating and managing a sustainable sporting future* (pp. 137–153). Routledge.

Pratt, A. C. (2005). Cultural industries and public policy: An oxymoron? *International Journal of Cultural Policy, 11*(1), 31–44.

Preuss, H. (2007). The conceptualisation and measurement of mega sport event legacies. *Journal of Sport & Tourism, 12*, 207–228.

Preuss, H. (2015). A framework for identifying the legacies of a mega sport event. *Leisure Studies, 34*, 643–664.

Prüschenk, N., & Kurscheidt, M. (2017). Do the Youth Olympic Games have the potential to shift perceptions of Olympism? Evidence from young people's views on Olympic values. *International Journal of Sport Management and Marketing, 17*(4–6), 351–380.

Rattansi, A., & Phoenix, A. (2005). Rethinking youth identities: Modernist and postmodernist frameworks. *Identity, 5*(2), 97–123. https://doi.org/10.1207/s1532706xid0502_2

Reis, A. C., de Sousa-Mast, F. R., & Gurgel, L. A. (2014). Rio 2016 and the sport participation legacies. *Leisure Studies, 33*(5), 437–453.

Ricordel, P. (2023). The circular heritage model of Paris 2024 and its possible local legacy perspective. *Local Economy, 38*(4), 405–417.

Rigney, A., & Erll, A. (2009). Introduction: Cultural memory and its dynamics. In A. Erll & A. Rigney (Eds.), *Mediation, remediation, and the dynamics of cultural memory* (pp. 1–11). de Gruyter.

Ritchie, B. W., Shipway, R., & Chien, P. M. (2010). The role of the media in influencing residents' support for the 2012 Olympic Games. *International Journal of Event and Festival Management, 1*, 202–219.

Roche, M. (2002). *Mega-events and modernity: Olympics and expos in the growth of global culture*. Routledge.

Roche, M. (2023). The Olympics and 'global citizenship'. In *The Olympics* (pp. 108–120). Routledge.

Rubim, A. A. C. (2013). Políticas culturais do governo Lula. In *Revista Lusófona de Estudos Culturais* (pp. 224–242).

Sakib, S. M. N. (2021). Level of political engagement in UK. *APSA Preprints*. https://doi.org/10.33774/apsa-2021-trtt9

Scheu, A., Preuß, H., & Könecke, T. (2021). The legacy of the Olympic Games: A review. *Journal of Global Sport Management, 6*(3), 212–233.

Scott, C. (2014). Legacy evaluation and London, 2012 and the Cultural Olympiad. *Cultural Trends, 23*(1), 7–17.

Seidl, M., Nagiller, R., Lang, A., Scheiber, S., & Schnitzer, M. (2021). Youth Olympic Games (YOG) 2012—Mission accomplished? A retrospective analysis of intangible legacies and the fulfillment of the YOG's goals. *Journal of Global Sport Management, 6*(3), 292–313.

Shipway, R. (2007). Sustainable legacies for the 2012 Olympic Games. *Journal of the Royal Society for the Promotion of Health, 127*(3), 119–124.

Silva, W. C. D., & Cerdan, L. M. (2014). Rio 2016: Os preparativos e desafios da cidade olímpica. *Turismo e Sociedade, 7*(1).

Sloam, J. (2007). Rebooting democracy: Youth participation in politics in the UK. *Parliamentary Affairs, 60*(4), 548–567.

Sloam, J. (2011a). Introduction: Youth, citizenship and politics. *Parliamentary Affairs, 65*(1), 4–12.

Sloam, J. (2011b). 'Rejuvenating democracy?' Young people and the 'Big Society' project. *Parliamentary Affairs, 65*(1), 90–114.

Sloam, J. (2014). 'The outraged young': Young Europeans, civic engagement and the new media in a time of crisis. *Information, Communication & Society, 17*(2), 217–231.

Smith, N., Lister, R., Middleton, S., & Cox, L. (2005). Young people as real citizens: Towards an inclusionary understanding of citizenship. *Journal of Youth Studies, 8*(4), 425–443.

Smith, A., Gold, J. R., & Gold, M. M. (2024). Olympic urbanism: Past, present and future. *Planning Perspectives, 39*(3), 487–499.

Staalstroem, J. (2021). *The influence of the Youth Olympic Games education program on athletes* (Doctoral dissertation).

Stålstrøm, J., Iskhakova, M., & Pedersen, Z. P. (2023). Role models and Athlete expression at the Youth Olympic Games as impactful sport communication practices. *International Journal of Sport Communication, 16*(4), 435–449.

Stockdale, L. (2012). More than just games: The global politics of the Olympic Movement. *Sport in Society, 15*(6), 839–854.

Swartz, S., & Arnot, M. (2014). Introduction: Youth citizenship and the politics of belonging: Introducing contexts, voices, imaginaries. In *Youth citizenship and the politics of belonging* (pp. 1–10). Routledge.

Szaniecki, B., & Silva, G. (2010). Megaeventos pontos de cultura e novos direitos culturais no Rio de Janeiro. In *Lugar Comum–Estudos de mídia, cultura e democracia* (pp. 31–32).

The Telegraph. (2009). *Brazil's weeping President Luiz Inacio Lula da Silva revels in 2016 Olympics vote*. The Telegraph 3 October [Online]. Retrieved September 28, 2019, from https://www.telegraph.co.uk/sport/olympics/news/6257463/Brazils-weeping-President-Luiz-Inacio-Lula-da-Silva-revels-in-2016-Olympics-vote.html

Thorpe, H. (2022). *Action sports and the Olympic Games: Past, present, future* (p. 327). Taylor & Francis.

Thorpe, H., & Wheaton, B. (2011). 'Generation X Games', action sports and the Olympic movement: Understanding the cultural politics of incorporation. *Sociology, 45*(5), 830–847.

Torres, C. R. (2012). *On the merit of the legacy of failed Olympic bids*. International Olympic Committee.

Tsekoura, M. (2016). Spaces for youth participation and youth empowerment. *Young, 24*(4), 326–341. https://doi.org/10.1177/1103308815618505

Turino, C. (2018). *The point of Culture: Brazil turned upside down*. Calouste Gulbenkian Foundation, UK Branch.

UNESCO. (n.d.). *What is intangible cultural heritage?*. Retrieved from https://ich.unesco.org/en/what-is-intangible-heritage-00003

Van Dijck, J. (2007). *Mediated memories in the digital age*. Stanford University Press.

Veal, A. J., Toohey, K., & Frawley, S. (2012). The sport participation legacy of the Sydney 2000 Olympic Games and other international sporting events hosted in Australia. *Journal of Policy Research in Tourism, Leisure and Events, 4*(2), 155–184.

Vilutis, L. (2011). *Ação agente cultura viva: Contribuições para uma política cultural de juventude* (p. 111). Governo Federal.

Wallace, C. (2018). Youth, citizenship and empowerment. In *Youth, citizenship and empowerment* (pp. 11–31).

Watt, P. (2013). 'It's not for us' Regeneration, the 2012 Olympics and the gentrification of East London. *City, 17*(1), 99–118.

Weller, S. (2007). *Teenagers' citizenship: Experiences and education*. Routledge.

Wise, N., & Kohe, G. Z. (2020). Sports geography: New approaches, perspectives and directions. *Sport in Society, 23*(1), 1–10.

Wong, D. (2011). The Youth Olympic Games: Past, present and future. *The International Journal of the History of Sport, 28*(13), 1831–1851.

Zhong, Y., Fan, H., & Herrmann, P. (2022). The impact of the 2008 Beijing Olympic Games on China and the Olympic movement: The legacy. *The International Journal of the History of Sport, 38*(18), 1863–1879.

Zhou, R., Kaplanidou, K., & Chatziefstathiou, D. (2020). The case of two Youth Olympic Games. In *Routledge handbook of the Olympic and Paralympic Games.*

CHAPTER 2

The Olympics from Youth Perspective: A New Methodological Approach

Abstract This chapter outlines and describes the methodological approach applied in this book. It begins by explaining the reason why this research project was underpinned by a mixture of qualitative methods and modes of analysis and the importance of the research design put together to reflect the three main fields addressed and explored in the study (Media, Memory and Youth citizenship across the North–South divide).

Three research questions are put forward in order to contextualise the rationale and need for this study and, subsequently, the methods selected for this research. The chapter also explains, in detail, the importance of space, place and diversity when conducting research with young people in light of mega-events and identity constructions and how these aspects were carefully integrated into the methodology. Finally, but equally important, in the chapter I explain the ethical considerations taken on board when conducting the study, particularly with young people.

Keywords Methodology • Qualitative approaches • Media • Memory • Youth citizenship

The methodological approach of the study presented in this book is underpinned by a mixture of qualitative methods and modes of analysis. As a result, the methodology adopted here follows an interpretivist and

S. Borges Tavares, *Youth Policy, Citizenship Education and Olympic Games Legacies*, Mega Event Planning,
https://doi.org/10.1007/978-981-99-6579-3_2

constructivist and inductive approach with regard to the relationship between theory and research, wherein the former is generated out of the latter (Bryman, 2016, p. 23).

The research design was conceived in order to contemplate the three key areas that this study is concerned with, both from a theoretical and practical point of view which covers the following themes or theoretical areas: media, memory and youth citizenship. As a result, I employed data triangulation and a mixed methods approach, which is explained in more detail along the next sections, as a way forward to investigate the role of mega and mediatised events, like the Olympics, in young people's perceptions and enactments of national identity, as well as citizenship values. In addition, this book also unveils data that identifies ways in which young people relate to the Olympics from a legacy perspective. And finally, I explore the extent to which young people's memories and imaginaries in relation to the Olympics might provide a new conceptual framework for assessing and understanding their engagement with the legacies of these events.

At the core of these cross-examinations are the perceptions and subsequent citizenship values of young people from two different settings, who took part in this study. The aim, however, is not to make a comparative case study approach between the youth from London and youth from Rio de Janeiro. Instead, the methodological steps taken forward and explained in this book were put together in order to answer the above questions, but also to bring a diversity of views and topics from two global divided milieu. The element of memory and the idea of a mnemonic imagination (Keightley & Pickering, 2012) is explored methodologically in order to explore the participants' discursive views about the Olympics based on previous recollections from, for example, the World Cup.

Figure 2.1 outlines in a much clearer way the components and steps of the methodological approach, which will be expanded in the following sections.

Ethical Considerations

In order to conduct this research with young people, I had to take into consideration the different and potential challenges that could occur during the fieldwork in the two distinctive cities, London and Rio de Janeiro. This meant thinking carefully about how to get access to participants in safe environments for them, the conditions of spaces (e.g. schools, youth clubs and other spaces) where the research took place, and any issues that

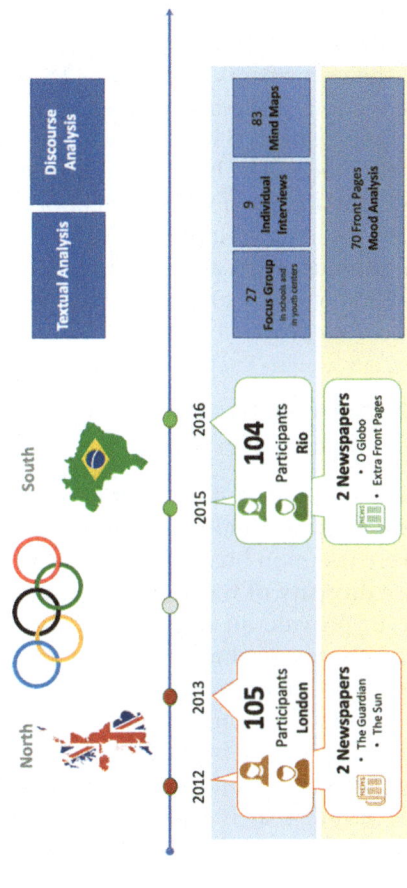

Fig. 2.1   Methodological approach

could come up during this process. The ethical practices of the project followed the university where the study was being done, namely the Ethical Guidelines with permission from the Ethical Committee responsible for this type of endorsement. As part of the process, an information sheet was produced for parents and schools explaining the aims of the research and the intended outcomes. In addition, consent forms were also sent out to parents and the schools in order to be signed off on behalf of the participants, where the participants were under 18 years old.

For ethical purposes, schools' and participant's names were kept anonymous throughout the entire study. The data was also transcribed from audio into text (word document—to be used later in NVivo, and in the case of Rio de Janeiro translated to English). Schools, youth clubs and community centres were labelled with letters for ease of identification, and participants were given a pseudonym as a means of ensuring anonymity. The whole process was conducted by following legislation on data protection and bearing in mind data protection and GDPR adherence.

Participants' Recruitment: Problematising Youth, Space and Place

The first and perhaps one of the most important parts of this study relates to how participants were recruited and what considerations (both ethical and methodological) were taken on board during this process. This aspect is key not only to ensure diversity of the sampling, which is important for this study, but equally to provide an opportunity for all young people whose ages and characteristics were aligned with the interests and aims of this research. Youth is seen as one of the most promising groups of society and one that holds the future of nations (Rafik & Belaadi, 2022). Having said that, explaining what one means by 'youth', for research purposes, is a complex task but nevertheless paramount to understand the impact of this research within the group that is under study (Cieslik & Simpson, 2013, p. 3). The concept itself overlaps with other concepts, such as childhood or adolescence. The United Nations[1] defines youth as those between 15 and 24, whereas childhood is often defined as anyone under 18 years old. In any case, youth is an 'elastic' concept and a social construct, as it

---

[1] According to the United Nations, there is not universally agreed definition of the age group for youth. Yet, for statistical purposes the UN defines youth as anyone aged between 15 and 24 years old. Find out more here: https://www.un.org/en/global-issues/youth

may cover different interpretations and overlaps across ages, nations and, more importantly, is seen as a product of history (France et al., 2020). In this book, I focus on the sociological interpretations of youth, concerning mainly the relationship between young people and their broader contexts by bearing in mind that the social construct of youth implies that being young in one country is not necessarily the same as another country. This is particularly evident when we consider the historical, cultural and social factors between the North–South divide.

As such, further attention is given to the sampling of participants in terms of diversity, by ensuring that they come from different walks of life, as well as socio, spatial and economic contexts as described below. Yet, by considering youth from a sociological perspective rather than a biological one means that although age is somewhat relevant, we are prone to look beyond this category and instead consider the different considerations given to youth in the settings where the research took place.

Criteria for Young People's Recruitment

I relied on two criteria to set out and define the age group of the pool of participants. The first one attended the temporal occurrences of the events: the Summer Olympic and Paralympic Games in 2012 and 2016. Given that this book investigates young people's memories and imaginaries of this mass media event taking place every four years, such time-span had to be factored into the equation when selecting the age of participants. This meant that participants could neither be too young nor too old within the various categorisations of youth, so that they could critically engage in the discussions about the Olympics. As a result, the age bracket of 11–26 years old proved to be a good choice for participants to engage critically with the topics and draw on their recollections and imaginaries in relation to the Games. The idea of memory as one of the strands of this research implies looking at what memory is constructed not just from the young participants' perspective but also from the Olympics in regard to its role to the heritage-based approach to sport (Violette & Attali, 2020). For some of these authors, 'sport is a phenomenon of cultural hybridity' (ibid., 1077), leading to various outcomes at a local or community level. The IOC has always had in mind the impact that the Games could have in terms of heritage memory, be it personal or mediated. According to Cashman (2006), memory plays an important role in the Olympics industry and the host cities, given that the chances of the Games taking place in the same city in a short to medium time is very unlikely. This suggests looking at the intangible legacies, from a perspective of what memories or recollections young people may have of the Games but also from the viewpoint of the IOC heritage policy as the values disseminated by the Olympic Movement. Within the different approaches, be it local or national, youth volunteering is one aspect that has been argued as positive in terms of impacting towards long-lasting legacies. As a result, the participants recruitment was done by taking into account the diversity of activities these young people may have been involved before, during or after the Games. Studies in this field suggest that the volunteering programmes both at the Youth Olympic Games and the Summer Olympics are seen as leaving a long-lasting and positive impact, particularly for the young people, underpinned by the memories and expectations they take from the experiences as part of their autobiographical memory in relation to the Olympic Movement (Wang et al., 2023). Such arguments support the importance of exploring a diversity of views and recollections from the participants by allowing such voices to give shape and form to what could be interpreted as their understanding of legacies.

The spatial and temporal elements of the Olympics play a key role in how cities and historical events are remembered and situated within politics of memory and in how young people see their local settings being transformed. The Winter Olympic Games in Sarajevo in 1984 is an example of how the event marks a period of contestation. Following the siege of the city eight years after the Games, the remaining heritage of the Olympics, like the Olympic hotel, become symbols of war and disruption in the landscape of the city. Yet, Sarajevo is one of the cities in the Balkans privilege for having host the Games and therefore able to capitalise on the commemoration of that fact, by using the heritage both material and immaterial to project the legacy of a space of 'authentic imagination' which should be imprinted in the map of the Olympics (Husukić & Zejnilović, 2020, p. 15). In this case, the two spaces where the participants come from are relevant bearing different cultural and historical specificities which will be reflected on their recollections and imaginaries of the Games. The idea that these young participants may have of certain sports may vary depending on their experiences but also on the settings and the historical contexts they are inserted. For example, in the case of Brazil, as I will be able to explore further in the following chapters, football is seen as a sport of contestation and dispute in terms of gender and class. The body of scholarship conducted in this area suggests that oral histories of players are methodological relevant, as it is through these voices that is it possible to change the content of certain narratives by shifting the attention to the people telling the stories (Thompson, 2002) as opposed to the institutions or the media. One example of this is the work on the memories of women's football in Brazil who played for the National Team and the Olympics. The research conducted in this area points to a perception that football in their country has been developed from top down to bottom. Their memories about these experiences are based on the differences between the national team (which is well organised and structured) against the disorganised chaos of the clubs (Oliveira Souza & Capraro, 2020). I draw upon these works in order to demonstrate the extent to which memory politics and collective or public memory of certain sport events are relevant when considering the criteria for young people's recruitment and the different contexts, both temporal and spatial they are recruited from. Given that memory is one of the key thematic areas that I wish to explore, the recruitment of participants from different local areas and regions within the cities is equally paramount to express a diversity of experiences, first-hand or mediated memories or imaginaries of the Games. In the case of Brazil, the expectation in relation to the event, which was about to happen, are claimed as intrinsically related to the socio, political, cultural and economic contexts of each young participant. Hence, diversity is equally key in this sense, in order to give us a variety of views on the intangible legacies of the Olympics, or based on past experiences of other mega-events (which is the case of Rio de Janeiro).

The second criterion was based on the conceptualisation of youth as a transitional process and one that is very much conditioned by different meanings, places and belongings. I consider youth by putting instead the emphasis on location, the socioeconomic and historical situation, and the 'variations that exist in the treatment of youth' (Beauvais et al., 2001, p. 4) in each setting. Accordingly, I embrace the concept of youth in line with how 'different understandings of society divide the social space into different groups' (Jorgensen & Phillips, 2002, p. 46). Thus, this book considers a plethora of ages within the age bracket of 11–26 years old, across the different spatial contexts in which the fieldwork took place, in order to conform to distinct sociological definitions of youth. As a result, youth performances and constructions of identities are viewed in addition to the temporality and biological perspectives ascribed to this group. In its place, they are contemplated as interwoven with notions of space, place and globalisation (Farrugia & Wood, 2017). These concepts are of great importance for this book, and form the basis of the definition and conceptualisation of youth citizenship, as they suggest that young people need to be examined within their contextualised social, political and economic relations with societies, rather than as a category.

The target audience of this study involved a wide pool totalling 209 young people aged between 11 and 26 years old from the two cities of London and Rio de Janeiro. Further attention was given to the historical and spatial specificities of the places the participants came from within their own cities, which as I already referred above it will have implications on their views, recollections and expectations of the Games.

In the case of London, the recruitment of participants was aimed at three distinct pools of participants. The first pool of participants came from an educational context, from four schools and two youth clubs (Table 2.1). The second pool came from a group of students in Higher Education, who were part of a BA programme (Table 2.2). The last pool represents different participants without any pre-existing connections, but who came forward through a snowball sampling of different contacts and who showed an interest in participating in this study (Table 2.4). The last pool was also the result of a snowball effect through which participants were recruited based on the recruitment poster that was put together for this purpose, including through other contacts.

In addition to schools and youth clubs, there was also an intention to involve participants from schools that were part of the London Olympic Educational programme—Get Set[2]—in order to compare the participants'

Table 2.1 Information of participants from London schools

School	N. participants	Dates	Age range (years)
A	14	22/01/14	12–17
B	5	3/12/2015	11–17
C	6	17/11/15	16–18
D	9	29/04/15	16–18
E	11	20/05/14	11–14
F	38	9/10/14 and 23/10/14	14–18

[2] The Get Set Programme was the official education programme of London 2012 Summer Olympic and Paralympic Games. The aim was to inspire and educate children aged between 3 and 19 years old all over the United Kingdom based on the Olympic values. These included excellence, friendship, respect, determination, inspiration, amongst other values. The programme reached out different schools across the United Kingdom with the aim of spreading the Olympic spirit and educate these young people about the Olympic values.

Table 2.2 Participants recruited from a higher education context

Participant pseudonym	Location by post code	Gender	Age
John	SE7 4XA	Male	Not provided
Kim	EC2A	Female	Not provided
Sarah	SE1 4XA	Female	18
Joanna	Not provided	Female	19
Charlotte	SE1 0FN	Female	19
Poppy	TW9 3BG	Female	Not provided
Jessica	Not provided	Female	18
Sophie	EN4 8PU	Female	21
Christina	Not provided	Female	20
Anna	Not provided	Female	19
Amelia	N1 5EJ	Female	20
Charles	Not provided	Male	Not provided
Melissa	Not provided	Female	Not provided
Lilly	WC1H 0AQ	Female	19
Olivia	SE1 9NQ	Female	Not provided

discourse around legacy with other young participants from other contexts, who were not engaged in such a programme. However, for confidentiality reasons, the London Organising Committee of the Olympic Games (LOCOG) was not unwilling to disclose the contacts of schools involved in the Get Set Programme Transforma.[3] In Rio de Janeiro, however, a list of some of the schools that were part of the Games' education programme was provided upon request.

The recruitment of participants took place in two phases, by employing a non-random sampling approach. The purpose was to get a substantial number of participants but equally to be able to make important insights while exploring the data from these two settings and contexts.

---

[3] Transforma (English = Transform) was the official education programme of the Rio de Janeiro 2016 Summer Olympic and Paralympic Games. Similar to London, the idea behind this education programme was to reach out to young people in Rio de Janeiro and share the values of the Olympic Movement. In the case of Rio de Janeiro, the programme was launched in 2013 in 15 schools in Rio and subsequently spread around the country. Events such as coaching sessions and sport festivals, were just some of the many initiatives undertaken as part of this programme. Official figures suggest that by the end of Rio's Olympic Games, over 6 million students from over 12,000 schools across the country had experienced new sports for the first time, thanks to the Transforma programme.

Sample Settings and Participants in the United Kingdom

Research Site 1: Schools and Youth Clubs
The following information (Table 2.1) summarises the sample settings and participants in the UK schools and youth clubs, which is followed by a more detailed explanation.

Table 2.1 provides further information about the participants who came from the four schools and the two youth clubs. Out of these 83 participants, 16 came from youth clubs. The decision for putting youth clubs together with the schools was due to the nature of the environments in which the sampling and data collection took place. Both schools and youth clubs are viewed, to some degree, as formal settings. It is important to mention that, as with many other contexts, researching in school environments has its advantages and disadvantages. On the one hand, it allows the researcher to easily gather participants from different age groups and social contexts in one place. Additionally, from the perspective of participant observation and for the purpose of conducting focus groups discussions, this type of setting is ideal. Yet, on the other hand, school environments often reinforce the underlying power dynamics between adults and children-young people. It has been argued that in these cases 'expectations are often compounded by a context in which adults are in control' (Hill, 2006, p. 81). I tried to mitigate this by using icebreakers and also introducing the researcher as a 'student' like them, rather than as a teacher.

Despite their different environments, youth clubs and secondary schools were often controlled and supervised by adults throughout the empirical work. This, among other aspects, is important to stress, particularly when undertaking qualitative research with young people. Accordingly, in youth and children's studies, little attention has been paid to the context in which the research takes place. As a result, the position of the researcher and the act of 'doing research' has largely been neglected (Buckingham, 1993). With that in mind, these aspects were taken into consideration, including the role and position of the researcher. One of the ways used to tackle this was the use of mind-map exercises as an icebreaker and important method of data collection amongst the young participants.

Two out of the four schools in Table 2.1 fall under the category of Academies. In the United Kingdom, Academies are state-funded schools, funded by the Department for Education (DfE) and run independent from local authority control.

The other remaining schools fall under the category of Foundations (School C) and Community Schools (School D). School C is located in the borough of Lambeth, Blackfriars, whereas school D, for boys only, is in the East End of London, serving the local community, which has the highest number of students with Bangladeshi backgrounds in London.

Youth Club B serves the local community of young people in Lambeth and offers a variety of activities from arts to sports. It focuses on the youth population of the area aged between 11 and 19 and up to 25 years old for those with disabilities. Out of the five young participants from this Youth Club, one had a disability. Youth Club E is located in central London and is specifically aimed for young people in the Holborn and Covent Garden area. Founded in 2005, the club has a strong ethos and focus on the local community, with projects and activities aimed at challenging negative pre-conceptions and encouraging young people to make a positive contribu-tion to their local communities. The club also challenges the idea of the area (Holborn and Covent Garden) as a 'wealthy' one, claiming instead that there can be high levels of deprivation and significant divergence between wealth and poverty in the same place.[4]

Research Site 2: University Context

Table 2.2 provides information about the sampling of participants who were undertaking a BA programme in the United Kingdom at the time of this study. The opportunity to interview these young people came through established contacts which resulted in a total of 15 participants. Gender, location and other contextual inputs from participants (e.g. ethnicity, nationality and cultural background) were all taken into consideration during the data analysis and analytical discussion.

Research Site 3: Participants from Other Contexts

The final pool of participants from London was arranged via colleagues and friends. Further information about these seven participants can be found in Table 2.3. Aged between 19 and 25 years old, all of these young people with the exception of one are female. The location varied from

---

[4] According to the London Datastore website, information on poverty in London between 2017 and 2018 indicated that the number of children in material deprivation was and is still higher in Inner London, when compared to other areas of the city (https://data.london. gov.uk/apps_and_analysis/poverty-in-london-2017-18/).

Table 2.3 London participants from other contexts

Sam	SE5 8AN	Female	25
Catherine	E1 1AF	Female	24
Serena	Not provided	Female	Not provided
Silvia	SE17 2SX	Female	19
Hannah	E6 1QP	Female	Not provided
Olivier	SE1 9NS	Male	19
Paula	SM3 8RY	Female	20

Table 2.4 Participant information from Rio de Janeiro's schools and youth

School	N. participants	Dates	Age range (years)
G	9	26/03/15	16–17
H	23	23/03/15	15–18
I	8	16/03/15	13–18
J	6	13/03/15	14–16
K	5	17/03/15	10–11
L	10	27/03/15	15–17
M	8	18/03/15	14–16
N	6	10/03/15	18–21

Table 2.5 Schools from Rio de Janeiro that participated in the Transforma Programme

School	N. participants	Dates
O	5	23/10/15
P	5	06/10/15
Q	17	10/08/15

South-East London (three participants) to East London (two participants), and the Sutton Area, South-West London, postcode SM (one participant).

Similar to the participant recruitment that took place in London, the empirical work and sampling from Rio de Janeiro involved schools, youth clubs (from local communities) and individual participants from other contexts. Table 2.4 shows the different areas and schools or community groups/clubs in which the fieldwork took place in Rio. As mentioned earlier, unlike London, it was possible to interview young people from three schools that participated in the Education Programme of the Rio Games—Transforma (see Table 2.5).

Sample Settings and Participants in Brazil

Research Site 1: Schools and Youth Clubs/Community Centres

A total of 75 respondents from the above schools in Rio de Janeiro participated in this study. Out of this total, 14 came from youth/community clubs, and 6 from educational organisations working with UNICEF Brazil. The remaining participants came from Estate Schools (47 young people) and a Private School (8 young people) (see Table 2.4). Table 2.5 shows those young participants whose schools were involved in the Transforma Programme (Educational Programme of Rio Organising Committee of the Olympic Games—ROCOG). These participants were put in a separate table (below) with the purpose to better visualise and contextualise the spatiality and subsequent narratives in relation to the Games. All of them are located in the metropolitan area of Rio de Janeiro, although not in the city centre—the schools are categorised by the government as Metropolitan areas I, II and IV of the Rio de Janeiro Estate. In addition to space, the Olympic rhetoric embedded in educational programmes like Transforma also pervades the discourse of these young people, including how they imagine the city and their own local settings.

Research Site 2: Schools That Took Part in the Transforma Programme

In addition to schools and youth clubs' environments, two young inhabitants of Rio de Janeiro, Ricardo, a son of a university teacher, living in the area of Santa Teresa,[5] who was about to enter going to university, and João, a university student, from a middle-class family living in the city centre, also participated in the study (see Table 2.6).

Table 2.6 Participants from other contexts in Rio de Janeiro

Participant pseudonym	Location/post code	Gender	Age
Ricardo	(Santa Teresa, RJ)	Male	16
Joao	Botafogo area, RJ	Male	20

[5] Once considered an upscale Rio de Janeiro's neighbourhood, Santa Teresa is nowadays popular for tourism and as a site of cultural interest.

Participants' Recruitment Overview

Diversity of space, place and participants' ages were all critical aspects for this study and for the different interpretations from young people regarding the social legacies left by the Olympic Games. This aspect is of utmost importance in both contexts given the discrepancies of class and economic structures that inevitably have implications on these young citizens' access to certain activities related to the Games, as well as their views and opinions of the same event. As a result, despite being from the same city, there were substantial differences within the same city, as well as important connections across the geographic contexts and backgrounds of the participants discussed further in this book. The gap identified in the literature review around the intricate yet significant connection between space and youth is carefully considered in this proposed methodological approach. In other words, the methodology is aligned with the idea that youth are 'constructions that vary according to the social processes that shape lives in different places around the world' (Farrugia, 2014, p. 609). Hence, diversity, in this sense, is critically reflected in how participants see the city and their sense of belonging, including their active participation within the same spaces. It allows, above all, the inclusion of different youth voices in one discursive space. Also, the age of the participants and their attitudes in relation to what they interpret as civic engagement in these different settings are all subject to different interpretations and definitions of youth. As a result, problematising youth and space during the participants' recruitment was critical for the subsequent discussions and analytical chapters of this book.

In addition to young participants, interviews also took place with people who were extremely helpful in providing additional information and who held substantial knowledge on this topic. These included individuals from organisations such as the International Olympic Committee (IOC) in Lausanne; the Local Organising Committees set up in each city; NGOs working with children, young people and citizenship projects; media organisations; and people working directly with young people in Brazil (see Table 2.7). Their views, ideas and inputs were taken on board throughout the study to highlight and support important discourses.

Table 2.7 Other contacts/contributions to the empirical work London/Rio de Janeiro

---

UK/London
- March 2013—London Organising Committee of the Olympic Games and Paralympic Games (LOCOG). Meeting with Nick Fuller (Head of Education for the London 2012 Olympic Games)

Brazil/Rio de Janeiro
- 9 March 2015—Meeting with Professor Regina de Assis (Former Professor at PUC and Secretary of Education, Rio de Janeiro)
- 9 March 2015—Meeting with Paulo Lima, Director of Viracao, an NGO, focused on educational and communication projects for young people in Brazil
- 11 March 2015—Rio Organising Committee of the Olympic and Paralympic Games (ROCOG). Meeting with Head of Education, Maria Berh; Strategic Communications Specialist, Carla Marques; and Education Coordinator, Ewerton Camargo
- 12 March 2015—Meeting with Gizele Martins, a young activist and favela resident, in favela *Complexo da Mare*
- 19 March 2015—Meeting with Professor Alessandra Alde, from the Media Department, Estate University of Rio de Janeiro, UERJ
- 24–25 March—Meeting with Executive Director, Antonio Silva and Finance Director Miriam Pragita from ANDI (Communication and Rights, Brazil) NGO based in Brasilia

---

MEDIA SAMPLING: WHAT DOES THE NEWS TELL US?

In addition to participants' data, a small sample of media was analysed with an aim to establish meaning between fragments of the participants' discourses (on their memories and expectations) and the media representations at the same time. This was a way of triangulating the data in order to validate the participants' accounts of their memories and imaginaries, as well as ensuring a subsequent analytical enrichment of the findings (Deacon et al., 2021, p. 135).

Two national daily newspapers were selected from each country, based on circulation rate, format and political alignment. In the United Kingdom, the *Guardian/Observer* and the *Sun's* front pages, spanning from 27 July to 13 August 2012, which covered the London 2012 Olympic Games period, were precisely selected for this study.[6] In Brazil, the front pages of

---

[6]To get a diverse and contrasting sample of content, the selection of newspapers' front pages was carried out on the basis of circulation rate, format, and political stance. In the case of the United Kingdom, and according to Newsworks (the marketing body for national newspapers—see Fig. 2.2) the Sun appears as the top newspaper by circulation rate, reaching 1,302,951 within the UK newspaper market. Considered a tabloid newspaper, the *Sun* was

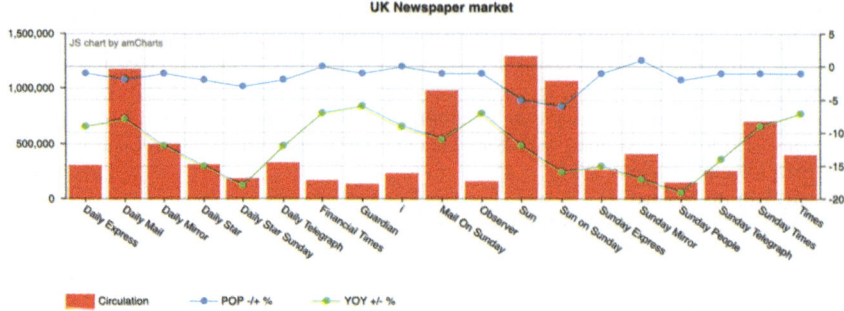

Fig. 2.2   UK Newspaper Circulation (source: Newsworks, n.d., n.p.)

O Globo and *Extra* were collected between 20 February and 10 March 2015, thus covering a two-week period before fieldwork in Rio de Janeiro.

In the case of the United Kingdom (Fig. 2.2), given that the aim was to explore participants' recollections of the London 2012 Olympic Games, the front pages covered the period spanning the duration of the Games. In total, 70 newspapers' front pages were examined (34 from the United Kingdom and 36 from Brazil) (Fig. 2.3).

Although young people are seen as increasingly shifting their news consumption towards the digital realm (Bakker & De Vreese, 2011; Casero-Ripollés, 2012) newspapers (in paper format) continue to play a significant part in the logic of media convergence (Jenkins, 2004). Based on their circulation and recent transition to online platforms, an analysis of these newspapers' front pages will be provided along the media assessment, given that the content was also displayed at the time online, and across different platforms. In other words, the 'online news services often largely mimic the content of original versions' (Tewksbury & Althaus, 2000, p. 458) and, faced with the impossibility of grasping all participants' media consumption, the front pages of these newspapers reflected, by and large, what also was circulated in the media (Chadwick, 2017), as part of what is considered a cultural logic of media convergence (Jenkins, 2004, p. 34).

selected in this case for its political stance (conservative), format (tabloid) and circulation rate (number one amongst UK daily newspapers). The *Guardian*, on the other hand and by contrast, despite not being considered the top choice in terms of readership or circulation rates, was selected given its political stance (centre-left, or liberal), format (broadsheet) and circulation rate (top newspaper with these characteristics).

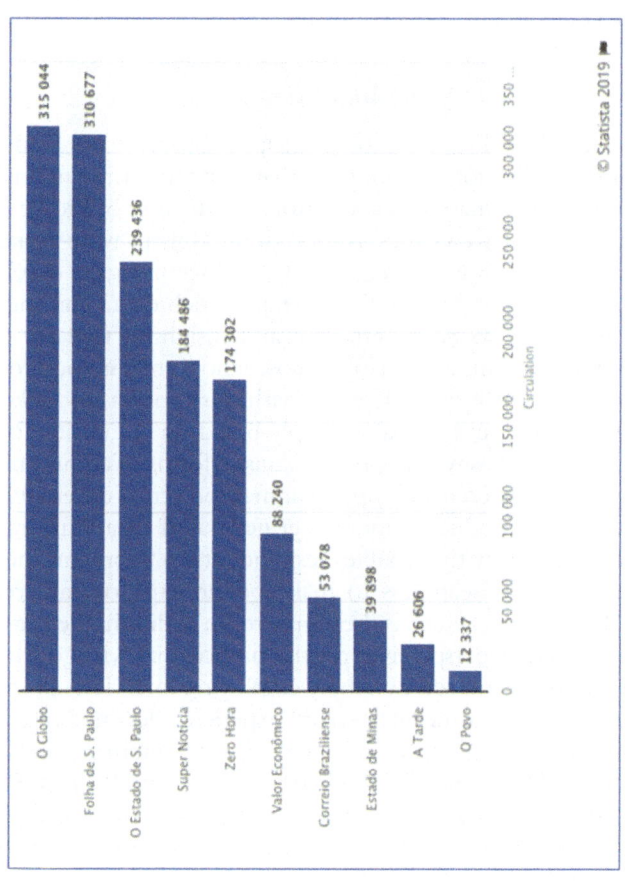

Fig. 2.3 Circulation of newspapers in Brazil

DATA COLLECTION

Mind-map exercises, and both individual and semi-structured focus group interviews and questionnaires, were the selected methods to collect data from participants. In addition, media content from selected front pages of two newspapers in each of these countries were also collected.

Mind-Map Exercises

In the case of schools and youth clubs, participants were encouraged to draw or write the first recollections—memories that came into their minds (in the case of London) or imaginaries—expectations (in the case of Rio de Janeiro) in relation to the respective Games. Although mind maps were initially used as an icebreaker and a warmup exercise to further instigate debate, they turned out to be incredibly useful for generating rich data. This method of data collection proved to be an effective and insightful tool for the first encounter with participants as it enabled those who were less vocal to express their views in a different format. The aim with this tool was to look beyond the notion of discourse and narrative simply based on linguistic modes and instead to include visual as well as other linguistic forms of communication.

Mind maps are considered a very popular method across different research fields and known for producing more user-generated data than traditional research methods in a way that enables respondents to 'represent their experiences while assisting researchers to make better sense of gathered data' (Wheeldon, 2010, p. 88), which is the aim here. In addition, the use of mind maps provides different perspectives on the participants' view of the world that could otherwise be missed by simply employing interviews or questionnaires, as they 'allow for a means to share experience less mitigated by linguistic constructions, culturally grounded understandings, and mutual accommodations' (Habermas, 1976, cited in Wheeldon, 2011, p. 510) and demonstrate how participants link knowledge to experience (Daley, 2004).

As I will be able to demonstrate along the book, not only were mind maps a very useful real-time transcription tool, allowing us to grasp preconceived ideas about the topic being researched (Tattersall et al., 2007), but they also offered a great exercise for instigating participants' memories. Existing research using this method suggests that it may, 'prompt research participants and unlock unique memories of past participant experiences' (Legard et al., 2003, p. 148). Mind maps also allowed participants to better 'recall, organize, and frame their reflections of past events' (Wheeldon, 2011, p. 509) (Figs. 2.4 and 2.5).

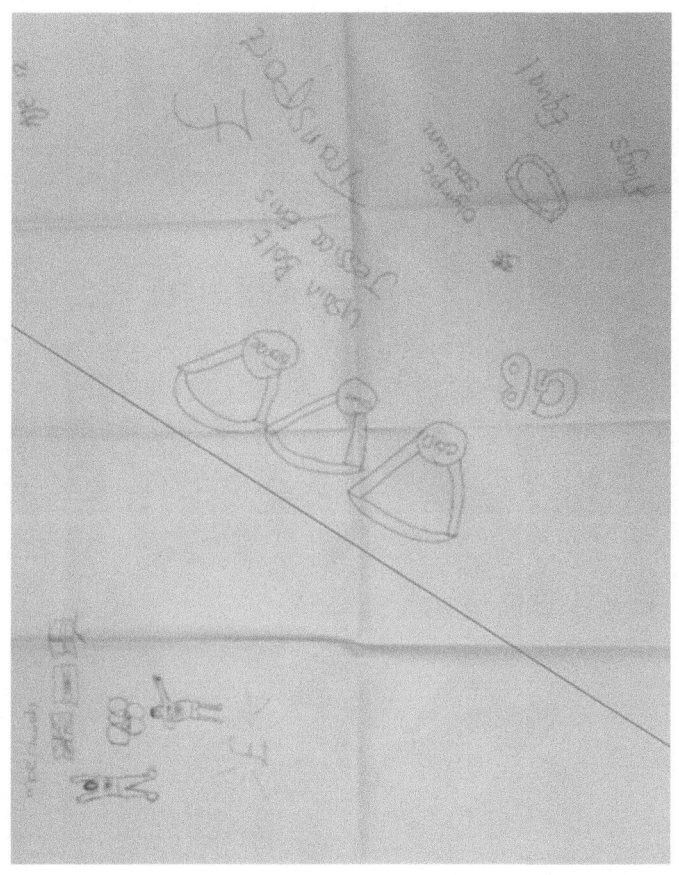

Fig. 2.4 Example of a mind-map exercise conducted with participants from London

Fig. 2.5 Example of a mind-map exercise conducted with young people during the fieldwork in Brazil

Focus Group Interviews

Following the mind-map exercises, and depending on the size of the classes, in groups of four or five, participants were asked questions based on an initial script prepared for this purpose. Some of the questions were adapted to attend to the data from the drawings and other substantial information that participants previously added during the mind-map exercise. This meant that the approach to the focus group interviews was both 'research constituted' and 'preconstituted' (Deacon et al., 1999, p. 65). Although a script with key questions to follow throughout the focus groups interviews was prepared in advance, the optional semi-structured interviews after the focus groups were less structured and added richness to the data. Both the focus groups and the interviews enabled some of the themes that were brought up in the mind-map exercise to be further explored in more detail. By employing mind-map exercises ahead of the focus groups in school settings, I attempted to offer a mixed-methods approach to data collection, suitable for a range of participants. In other words, I tried widen the level of participation and ensure the inclusion of young participants during different levels of the discussions. Whilst some of the participants felt more comfortable talking about their memories and imaginaries, others were perhaps more inclined to express themselves in writing or by drawing.

The focus group interviews took place in schools or youth clubs/community contexts, both in London and Rio de Janeiro. In groups of four to six, participants were encouraged to discuss different topics centred on their memories and imaginaries of the Olympic Games.

Individual Interviews

Individual interviews took place in two different scenarios. The first set took place in schools after the focus groups. Here, participants were invited to participate after being briefed on the purpose and length of the interviews. Unfortunately, school participants were not very receptive, and, as a result, it was not possible to proceed with individual interviews after the focus groups in some schools, mainly due to school constraints at that time. Although I had the parents' and schools' consent to proceed with the individual interviews for all the participants, this was only possible in other settings, for example, when I applied questionnaires with participants from different contexts. One of the reasons behind this approach was to contradict the view that researching children and young people is often conducted 'on them' rather than 'with them' (Freeman & Mathison, 2009, p. 1). Also, the aim was to ensure that those who were interviewed were, in fact, interested in the topic and genuinely wished to contribute to the study.

Questionnaires

Questionnaires were applied to collect data from participants in very specific contexts, such as when it was not possible to meet them in person and videoconferencing was not an option, or when they refused to participate in focus groups, but were still interested in taking part in the research. This method offered the opportunity to gather information in a way that would otherwise have been difficult. Also, questionnaires served as an additional supportive method by offering different responses about the same topic, drawing on the idea that 'when quantitative and qualitative approaches are used methodologically in combination with each other, the resulting analysis is invariably stronger' (Deacon et al., 1999, p. 134).

In the case of the schools in Rio de Janeiro that participated in the Olympics Transforma programme, confirmation of the interviews with students was granted close to the end of the fieldwork. In order to maximise data obtained the questionnaires were sent to these schools via a government entity that worked as an intermediary. The questionnaires were sent out by email to the department of the Ministry of Education of Brazil, and subsequently forwarded to the schools and after completion sent by to us scanned.

The same approach was used with the London participants from the Higher Education Context and with those who were interviewed individually, but not in a focus group format. In the case of participants from the Higher Education context, data collection took place during a university class. The nine participants who responded to the questionnaires were in a class setting, and given the time and space limits, it was not possible to probe them further on their answers.

On the other hand, the participants from London and Rio de Janeiro, outside of any educational context, who offered to take part in this study (Tables 2.3 and 2.6), not only completed the questionnaires but were subsequently individually interviewed. This added positively to the data as well as the study given that it was possible to expand on some of the answered topics from the questionnaires, in the same way as was done with the mind maps and focus groups.

DATA ANALYSIS

Given that this is a qualitative study, the approach to data analysis is also aligned with the nature and aims of the investigation. Three modes of analysis are applied in order to assess the different samples of data: discourse analysis, textual analysis and semiotics. I start by explaining the option of using discourse analysis which is seen as central to understanding youths' expressions and ideas of legacy around the Games.

Discourse Analysis

Discourse analysis is employed to examine and make sense of participants' narratives in relation to their memories and imaginaries of the Olympic Games. I focus specifically on the performative function of language and narratives and how these are shaped by participants' mediated or first-hand mnemonic experiences. In addition, I also look at the implications of such discourses with regard to multiple views of society, including civic engagement with the world. Discourse is therefore understood here as deeply intertwined with the 'social', where the 'discursive and the social mutually inform and mutually act upon each other' (Deacon et al., 1999, p. 147).

Despite the different levels of discourse addressed in this context, I put the emphasis 'on the practices of citizenship on the ground' (Fairclough et al., 2006, p. 98) because it is an approach that not only has been contested in theory and practice but equally claimed as significant for citizenship studies. In this book I will analyse the data from a variety of sources, such as the data resulting from focus group and individual interviews, as well as questionnaires.

Three levels of data were analysed drawing on social constructionist approaches to discourse. The first was collected from the focus group interviews undertaken in each school/youth club. The second level of data was from the individual semi-structured interviews with individual participants. The final level of data related to the questionnaires sent to participants, which produced written text.

Approaching the Data from a Textual and Semiotics Analysis

Textual analysis and semiotics were two modes of data analysis used in this research to interpret the drawings and texts produced by participants during the mind-map exercises. They were also used to examine the media content, specifically what I refer to in this book as 'media moods' from the selected newspapers' front pages.

Textual analysis was employed for the mind maps and the newspapers' front pages because the examination of such texts is arguably equally significant to establish connections between the role of the media and the participants' discursive memories and imaginaries (Bogart, 1984; Zelizer, 1992; Frosh, 2011; Garde-Hansen, 2011).

A thorough examination of the drawings and words from the mind maps was conducted, by employing a semiotic approach to text. Semiotics or semiology as 'the study of the sign and the way it works' (Fiske, 2010, p. 38) was exceptionally useful to help me understand how meaning was generated through signs (e.g., participants' drawings, and newspaper images or headlines).

The first level of this analysis consisted of identifying recurrent drawings or words/texts emerging from the mind maps and then subsequently grouping them according to codes or themes. The second level of analysis involved a deeper analysis of the data that was not necessarily repetitively coded but that stood out as intrinsically relevant to my research questions. For example, drawings or texts relating to national, local, or transnational identity, and those that suggested civic engagement conjectures, were extrapolated and examined individually using the same interpretive approach.

Textual analysis and semiotics were equally used in order to examine the selected front pages of newspapers from the United Kingdom and Brazil. Given that this study focuses on a mass media event and young people's perceptions, I felt the need to understand the relationship between media circulation and participants' views at specific times. As opposed to a quantitative content analysis approach to media data, textual analysis and semiotics proved to be more appropriate for this study.

All in all, textual and semiotic analysis enabled us to understand the ideologies, values and beliefs of these societal groups (Shils, 1961), as well as the historical and cultural specificities reflected in the newspapers' front pages (Fürsich, 2009). This type of media analysis proved to be equally critical as part of the modes of analysis and methodologies, as it linked specific arguments from participants' memories and imaginaries as mediatised and influenced by media consumption. By representing themselves as 'a discursive moment between encoding and decoding' (Fürsich, 2009, p. 238), media texts can no longer be 'understood as objectively examining or collecting data but as a "reading"' (ibid., 2009, p. 240). Certainly, newspapers were, in this case, amongst the different media that claimed to play an important role in representing the nation, both in relation to time and space.

BIBLIOGRAPHY

Bakker, T. P., & De Vreese, C. H. (2011). Good news for the future? Young people, Internet use, and political participation. *Communication Research, 38*(4), 451–470.

Beauvais, C., McKay, L., & Seddon, A. (2001). *A literature review on youth and citizenship*. CPRN Discussion Paper.

Bogart, L. (1984). The public's use and perception of newspapers. *Public Opinion Quarterly, 48*(4), 709–719.

Bryman, A. (2016). *Social research methods.* Oxford University Press.

Buckingham, D. (1993). *Reading audiences: Young people and the media.* Manchester University Press.

Casero-Ripollés, A. (2012). Beyond newspapers: News consumption among young people in the digital era. *Comunicar, 20*(39), 151–158.

Cashman, R. (2006). *The bitter-sweet awakening: The legacy of the Sydney 2000 Olympic Games.* Pan Macmillan.

Chadwick, A. (2017). *The hybrid media system: Politics and power.* Oxford University Press.

Cieslik, M., & Simpson, D. (2013). *Key concepts in youth studies.* Sage.

Daley, B. J. (2004). Using concept maps in qualitative research.

Deacon, D., Pickering, M., Golding, P., & Murdock, G. (1999). *Counting contents. Researching Communications.* Arnold.

Deacon, D., Pickering, M., Golding, P., & Murdock, G. (2021). *Researching communications: A practical guide to methods in media and cultural analysis.* Bloomsbury Publishing USA.

Fairclough, N., Pardoe, S., & Szerszynski, B. (2006). Critical discourse analysis and citizenship. In *Analysing citizenship talk* (pp. 98–123).

Farrugia, D. (2014). Towards a spatialised youth sociology: The rural and the urban in times of change. *Journal of Youth Studies, 17*(3), 293–307.

Farrugia, D., & Wood, B. E. (2017). Youth and spatiality. *Young, 25*(3), 209–218. https://doi.org/10.1177/1103308817712036

Fiske, J. (2010). *Introduction to communication studies.* Routledge.

France, A., Coffey, J., Roberts, S., & Waite, C. (2020). *Youth sociology.* Bloomsbury Publishing.

Freeman, M., & Mathison, S. (2009). *Researching children's experiences* (pp. 53–67). Guilford Press.

Frosh, P. (2011). Television and the imagination of memory: Life on Mars. In *On media memory* (pp. 117–131). Palgrave Macmillan.

Fürsich, E. (2009). In defense of textual analysis: Restoring a challenged method for journalism and media studies. *Journalism Studies, 10*(2), 238–252.

Garde-Hansen, J. (2011). *Media and memory.* Edinburgh University Press.

Habermas, J. (1976). Law as medium and law as institution. In G. Teubner (Ed.), *Dilemmas of law in the welfare state* (pp. 203–220). De Gruyter. https://doi. org/10.1515/9783110921526.203

Hill, M. (2006). Children's voices on ways of having a voice: Children's and young people's perspectives on methods used in research and consultation. *Childhood, 13*(1), 69–89.

Husukić, E., & Zejnilović, E. (2020). Beyond the Sarajevo 1984 Olympicscape: An evaluation of the Olympic villages. *Cities, 106,* 102924.

Jenkins, H. (2004). The cultural logic of media convergence. *International Journal of Cultural Studies, 7*(1), 33–43.

Jorgensen, M. W., & Phillips, L. J. (2002). *Discourse analysis as theory and method.* Sage.

Keightley, E., & Pickering, M. (2012). The mnemonic imagination. In *The mnemonic imagination* (pp. 43–80). Palgrave Macmillan.

Legard, R., Keegan, J., & Ward, K. (2003). In-depth interviews. In J. Ritchie & J. Lewis (Eds.), *Qualitative research practice: A guide for social research students and researchers* (pp. 138–169). Sage.

Oliveira Souza, M. T., & Capraro, A. M. (2020). Women's football in Brazil: Memories of the National Team's Athletes. *The International Journal of the History of Sport, 37*(5–6), 378–395.

Rafik, M., & Belaadi, B. (2022). The concept of youth: A sociological eye.

Shils, E. (1961). Centre and periphery. In *In the logic of personal knowledge: Essays presented to Michael Polanyi* (pp. 117–130). Routledge & Kegan Paul.

Tattersall, C., Watt, A., & Vermon, S. (2007). Mind mapping as a tool in qualitative research. *Nursing Times, 103*(26), 32–33.

Tewksbury, D., & Althaus, S. L. (2000). Differences in knowledge acquisition among readers of the paper and online versions of a national newspaper. *Journalism & Mass Communication Quarterly, 77*(3), 457–479.

Thompson, P. (2002). História oral e contemporaneidade. *Thomp, 5.*

Violette, L., & Attali, M. (2020). The Olympic memory: Institutional and heritage issues. *The International Journal of the History of Sport, 37*(11), 1066–1085.

Wang, Y., Derom, I., & Theeboom, M. (2023). Volunteering at the Olympic and Youth Olympic Games: More than a distant memory? *Journal of Global Sport Management, 8*(1), 361–385.

Wheeldon, J. (2010). Mapping mixed methods research: Methods, measures, and meaning. *Journal of Mixed Methods Research, 4*(2), 87–102.

Wheeldon, J. (2011). Is a picture worth a thousand words? Using mind maps to facilitate participant recall in qualitative research. *The Qualitative Report, 16*(2), 509–522.

Zelizer, B. (1992). CNN, the Gulf War, and journalistic practice. *Journal of Communication, 42*(1), 66–81.

CHAPTER 3

Case Study 1: Young Londoners' Memories of the 2012 Olympic Games

Abstract This chapter delves into the data analysis and findings from the case study of the Olympic Games in London 2012. It explores and discusses the results from the narratives of young participants of London in relation to their discursive memories and expectations of the Games. The findings and results are mixed between first-hand and mediated recollections, with the view of ascertaining the role of the media and memory in the construction of national, local and transnational identity aspects. As a result, the chapter is split between two samples of data: newspaper front pages (media aspect) and participants' discourses in relation to the past event of the Olympic Games. Questions about national, local and transnational identities are explored and interwoven with mediated and first-hand discursive memories from the young participants from London in light of the 2012 Olympic Games.

Keywords London 2012 • Memories • Youth recollections • Olympic Games • Youth identity • Civic engagement • Legacies

In this chapter I discuss some of the most important findings from two pools of data, by focusing on the memories of the London 2012 Olympic Games, specifically from the front pages of the selected newspapers and the young participants' narratives from London. I explored the data with the

© The Author(s), under exclusive license to Springer Nature   73
Singapore Pte Ltd. 2024
S. Borges Tavares, *Youth Policy, Citizenship Education and Olympic
Games Legacies*, Mega Event Planning,
https://doi.org/10.1007/978-981-99-6579-3_3

view of answering the research questions posed initially, and assess the different meanings ascribed to intangible legacy from the perspective of young people from London.

In the case of the United Kingdom, the front pages of the *Guardian/Observer* and the *Sun/The Sun* on *Sunday* were the newspapers selected for the media analysis. Both sets are daily newspapers, with a high volume of circulation, yet are of different formats and political stances, purposely to allow a variety of data. The following themes emerged from the textual analysis exercise conducted across the 36 front pages, during the 2 weeks corresponding to the 2012 Olympic Games in London:

1. The opening and closing ceremonies/spectacles;
2. The performance of British athletes versus other internationally acclaimed athletes;
3. Gold medals tally;
4. Expectations of the Olympic Games; and
5. Changes in the city/gentrification.

These topics are also, to some extent, implicitly or explicitly, embedded in the participant's views and narratives around the Olympic Games, at a national, local or even transnational level.

National, Local and Transnational Identities

In addition to national identity and citizenship portrayals, other key aspects are brought up here that have not been contemplated or explored in depth in traditional politics or citizenship scholarship and least in terms of youth policy around the Olympic Games. Although the literature on youth policy and the Olympic Games is mainly focused on the Youth Games claiming that the IOC always had the youth in mind as their primary focus, the fact is that their policies connected to young people are, by and large, concentrated on sports participation, dedicated to mitigating the problems of youth obesity and above all ensuring that young people are continuously engaged with the Olympics, in general (Chatziefstathiou, 2012).

On the contrary to what would be expected, the young participants in this study addressed the relevance of the Games for them in terms of bringing different people together, unlike other elite sporting events, and stressed the fact that the Games tend to reflect deep-rooted class systems in different countries. These points are of particular relevance given that lay people's perceptions (such as these young citizens) of national identity are considered a significant source of data (Jacobson, 1997, p. 181), especially in studies that aim to explore this complex topic from other perspectives. In this case, the excavations of their memories and imaginaries prompted participants to engage with the topic of national identity, in a critical and innovative fashion, as well as to voice their views about the Olympic Games in London. In other words, such an approach enabled an in-depth examination of young people's accounts, beyond the Olympics' topics already established in the policy agenda. John, for example, is one participant whose views appear to be in conflict with the messages and ideologies conveyed by the Games industry. In his statement, he also gives currency to different enactments and perceptions of national identity. In this case, he criticises the idea of countries hosting the Games for the sake of exhibiting the best of themselves, which is paradoxical when compared to the histories and legacies of the Olympic Games, including the discourse that views host cities as ideal platforms for demonstrating a national spectacle and display of pride (Tomlinson & Young, 2006):

> *I didn't feel proud for England. I don't really see the point because, you see, so many people make so much effort for just one week, for one event that you are going to have in another four years, in another country. I didn't feel proud, and I didn't really care. It's just a way of showing off their country. They make it to look good for something else, and I don't agree with that way of advertising the country. (John, London 20th May 2014)*

It is important to contextualise here that John belongs to a group of participants who were interviewed in a Youth Club group setting, located in central London. Also, although he is of British nationality, he nevertheless appears to be critical of the Olympics and of the idea of using the event as a platform for advertising the country, or, as he puts it, a 'way of showing off their country'. By 'their', he envisages other countries in addition to the United Kingdom that have hosted the Games in the past and followed the same pattern in attempting to display the best of themselves through the Games (Dayan & Katz, 1992; Roche, 2002). Despite the critical tone, this type of narrative resonates with feelings connected to national citizenship and identity. On the one hand, John is concerned about his country's image, by expressing a desire to belong within it. Yet, on the other hand, through his recollections of the 2012 Olympic Games in London, he describes how the country should be portrayed.

Moreover, John's excerpt connects with claims from other existing works that suggest that events like the Olympics are often used to produce an imagined idea of the nation through the opening and closing ceremonies (Roche, 2002, 2006; King, 2006). In this particular case, the London 2012 Olympic Games have been framed as a 'classic example of how an imagined community of Britishness gets fabricated and relayed' (Cohen, 2013, p. 23), an idea which aligns itself with John and other participants' views and which is important to explore in terms of expectations or memories of the Games.

Enactments of national identity are claimed to be grounded, above all, in notions of belonging (Triandafyllidou, 1998). Throughout this study, however, it appeared that they were similarly rooted in constructive yet critical views of the nation. Hence, the idea of belonging was deconstructed by some of the participants who, despite feeling proud of their local communities, cities or country were also critical of the same places and the government initiatives that affected them.

Implicit in John's rhetoric is the idea that the nation should serve its members' interests first, rather than just 'looking good for something else'. This conjecture also denotes the idea that, as a collective entity, the nation should 'look good' internally first before promoting itself externally.

While some respondents, like John, were very outspoken about the somewhat lack of pride in hosting the Games, others highlighted the potential of this mega-event in terms of bringing communities, families and countries together:

> They [athletes] represent your country; you don't have to be an elite to like sports, you can just, like … the Olympics is like that time that families and countries can be united, and accomplish something, like coming together. (Peter, London 3 December 2015)

Peter and other participants' similar discursive recollections echo ideas previously claimed within the body of scholarly literature that media events create a ritual amongst families, almost like a holiday whereby 'family members experience the event together, thus strengthening group memory and generational ties' (Dayan & Katz, 1992, p. 205). While this may have been hypothetically the case with some families across the United Kingdom, this participant points out something that is worth exploring further. He brings forward distinctive considerations around national and local identity and profound reflections on the meaning of belonging within but also beyond the nation and its geopolitical contexts. Speaking from the context of a Youth Club based in London, Peter refers to those who are not interested in sports (but could perhaps benefit from the Games from another perspective) stressing that, unlike other elite sports, in his view, the Olympics is an inclusive event that allows families and countries to be 'united'. The reference to the 'elite' appears to suggest that, contrary to what others might think, the Games are understood as overlooking class structures and thus providing an opportunity for countries and families to be united and to accomplish something together. This idea also connects to groundwork concepts of sports participation, fanhood and class, which ultimately are linked to a component of people's identity and a practice where one's stability is undisputed (Tamir, 2022).

Such enactments draw our attention to how these concepts operate within societies, such as in the case of the United Kingdom, where governments have utilised elite sporting to achieve a greater sense of national identity (Houlihan, 2002; Rowe, 2003). In the case of the London 2012 Olympic Games, to be more specific, the idea was to foster a sense of multi-ethnic youthful diversity supported by the power of sports and the values of Olympism, and with the view of a persistence in showcasing an image of multicultural Britishness (Silk, 2011).

The literature related to this area suggests that those with higher cultural capital are, indeed, less likely to be involved in what is designated as 'prole' sports (Wilson, 2002). To that end, Peter's memories of the London 2012 Olympic Games incite him to reflect upon these matters while simultaneously producing his own imaginary perspectives of belonging linked to viewing and participating in sports. Second, perceptions of belonging are reviewed by contemplating other depictions of identity beyond the national context. This means reinforcing the idea already stated by scholars in this field who claim that identities are not fixed but rather the result of social practices and processes subject to change (Du Gay, 1996; Maguire, 2011; Fina, 2012).

Some of the respondents' enactments of identity are situated at the interstices between local and national contexts, which is an interesting approach to consider while working in the development of youth policies. Nevertheless, given the ethnic and multicultural variety in British society, national identity is framed in this book as multifaceted and manifold (Asari et al., 2008). The nation is, very often, and as we can see from the participants' discourse, no longer contemplated as a site for 'the maintenance and continuous reproduction of the pattern of values, symbols, memories, myths' (Smith, 2000, cited in Asari et al., 2008, p. 2), with implications for individuals with the same heritage, values, memories and traditions. This is particularly the case for young citizens like Assad (see below) who, as a young Somalian living in the United Kingdom, finds himself negotiating meanings and feelings of his identity between his country of birth and country of residence:

> *Obviously, I am Somalian, so I don't think there was a [proud] feeling like that but obviously, my family and a lot of Somalian families do watch the Games because of Mo Farah and I was watching the race. I felt proud but at the same time disappointed because he was not running for his own country. I am still happy for him. (Assad, London, 3 December 2015)*

This type of transnational remembrance helps Assad to reconfigure his sense of belonging beyond the national frame (Assmann, 2014). In other words, it fosters a narrative that opens up the possibility to think about citizenship in terms of other forms of belonging, cultural identification and solidarity (Assmann, 2014, p. 546). In this case, Assad recalls that he did not feel particularly proud of London hosting the Games, yet his feelings changed upon seeing Mo Farah's performance. The use of the adverb 'obviously' is associated with national identity and the participant's affinity with Somalia, given the athlete's nationality, too.

Assuming that 'a lot of Somalians' watched the Games because of Mo Farah is also, in this specific case, a symbolic and discursive form of expressing transnational identity between British and Somalian identification. As explained in the literature review, sports are viewed as playing an important role in the formation of national identity (Maguire, 2011, p. 981).

The controversial expression—'Tebbit Cricket'[1] test—explains how, in the past, unspoken assumptions were made about one's sense of belonging and identity (in this case related to cricket). These have subsequently been subject to scrutiny in discussions of national identity, especially for people like young Assad, who may have two nationalities and yet feel both British and Somalian. As a British athlete, but of Somali ancestry, the appearance of Mo Farah challenges notions of English heterogeneity, an element that is still frequently deployed in sporting events. This also

---

[1] The Tebbit Cricket Test, or cricket test, was a controversial expression coined by British politician Norman Tebbit in 1990. It implied testing the loyalty of mainly South Asians and Caribbean immigrants in relation to the English national cricket team as a measure of fidelity and assimilation into the British culture (Fletcher, 2012).

supports what some scholars argue to be the 'matrix of social relations of power which in turn shapes the multiplicity of identities' (Birrell, 1988, cited in Gibbons & Malcolm, 2017, p. 204), particularly in mega sporting events, with the presence of international athletes of various ancestries. In this case, Assad sees Mo Farah as more Somalian than British, which could be explained as a self-contemplation of his own national identity, and if you like pride, given that he has British citizenship but is of Somali nationality.

In a similar vein, other challenging expressions about national identity emerged from participants' recollections of the Games. In the case of Hannah (see below), her memories of the Games prompted her to reflect on aspects of equality and opportunities for different nations:

Impact on society? The whole concept is meant to be unifying so I guess it is about bringing different countries together. I don't think they maintain that feeling. Not really. One big issue with the Olympics is that there is a lot of countries, like I mention, the flag bearing. There is a lot of countries, I am originally from Bangladesh and I mean the UK has loads of athletes and then you have maybe three from Bangladesh walking behind and it is just …. this whole thing is about unity and equality but it is really not equal because not every country has equal opportunities to train athletes you know… So they might have the athletes but [are] not given the same opportunity, so I know it is a bit off topic but it is important. (Hannah, London 26 July 2016)

On the contrary, Hannah's views are not 'off topic' when it comes to the focus of this study. While remembering the Olympic Games, she finds herself deeply contemplating the legacies, values and whole purpose of the event. The fact that she is originally from Bangladesh could, arguably, be one of the reasons why she paid more attention to certain aspects of the Games in comparison to other participants. By interrogating ideals that are intrinsic to the Olympic Games' legacy and values, Hannah draws attention to countries that perhaps do not have the same economic or social capacity to train their athletes. She problematises the idea of parity when it comes to the performances of countries and the gold medal tally in a way that reveals a critical understanding of the world and of how globalised mega-events, like the Olympics, operate at an international level. However, as a young British citizen, living in London, with a Bangladeshi cultural heritage, Hannah utilises both 'our country' and 'Newham' as expressions to evoke her identity simultaneously as British and a London/ Newham citizen.

From parts of Hannah's discourse, it is possible to note that she is engaged with the social and economic differences that permeate the city of London and supports the idea of Newham being chosen for the Games as opposed to other boroughs of London due to the economic and social circumstances. Although words like 'our country' and 'us' (Newham) are used interchangeably to ascertain national and local identity, it is the local in this case that appears to be of greatest significance in Hannah's discourse. Three different aspects inherent to identity performances are identified in this statement, supporting the view of youth performances as multiple in their forms (Lister et al., 2003) and relevant for understanding the local as a site of multiple disputes with the global city (Cohen & Ainley, 2000). The first performance relates to the nation, the second to the city of London, and the third to the borough Newham. Within these three spaces of belonging, the borough of Newham stands out as 'home'. As per Hannah's statement, it is not just the nation, but the sense of community felt in her borough during the Games that meant a great deal to her, which shows the extent to which her experiences and memories add significantly to the complex mosaic of different public spheres (Keane, 1995).

Depictions of national, local and transnational identity emerge as fluid and overlapping in some participants' recollections and imaginaries (Keane, 1995; Bauman, 2013). Yet, in this context, it seems that the dichotomy between national and local is often negotiated, attending to the importance given to the lived experiences and social circumstances of each participant. In the case of Hannah, it becomes evident that the local context of Newham is more significant when compared to the national contexts of the United Kingdom or Bangladesh. Such a sense of belonging is arguably driven—at least in part—by the Olympic legacy and the city planning for the 2012 Games. As mentioned before, the bid for the London 2012 Games involved, amongst other things, a plan to regenerate the city with a focus on the borough of Newham, where the Olympic Park was located (Imrie et al., 2009). Hence, for some of the young residents in these boroughs, like Hannah, local identity was more accentuated during this period due to the impact of the Olympic Games on their lives. On the other hand, place identity is also bound up with aspects related to the local community rather than the population of the country. In the case of Hannah, it appears that local and community identity in connection to Newham was already a driving force of pride before the Games. She begins her narrative by describing her nationality as Bangladeshi but ends up focusing on her 'home', which she attributes to the borough of Newham. This last aspect is equally relevant to make sense of place-making and cultural policies when planning events such as this one.

Displays of national identity and citizenship, on the other hand, are also evident throughout the participants' discursive recollections of the Olympic Games. One of the elements identified in the data is the simultaneous and interchangeable use of the word British and/or English as part of their identification with the nation. Similarly, drawings of the Union Jack and England's national flag, along with the use of words like 'British GB team' in the mind maps are examples of how, for some young respondents, senses of national identity and citizenship shifted between these two representations.

These above drawings from the mind-map exercises express powerful and symbolic representations of national belonging and reflect as well the importance of the nation, in light of this mega-event, for some participants. In fact, flags are viewed as an important part of people's cultural identity and an expression of diverse symbolic and political connotations as well as emotional power (Eriksen & Jenkins, 2007, p. 1). Having said that, little attention has been paid to the political and emotional elements displayed in flags in the field of nationalism research (Eriksen & Jenkins, 2007, p. 2), which opens up an opportunity to further explore the meanings attached to these young participants' national identity and contribute to a better understanding of their interpretations. In the case of the Union Jack and English flags, despite having different meanings, these often co-exist due to their historical context. With their respective distinctiveness and historical values, the two flags also denote different ideas of national belonging from the participants' viewpoints, who may or may not be aware of it. While the UK flag represents a union of different nations, the flag of England, on the other hand, has long been associated with nationalistic interpretations. Various scholars claim that sometimes, and particularly in sporting events, this can be a sign of a new localism. King (2006), for example, explains how until 1990 England fans preferred to use the Union Jack flag in football competitions, with their clubs' names printed on it, but then replaced it with the St. George's Cross.

Historically, flags have always been associated with nationalist symbolism, particularly in the context of sports and competitions (Tomlinson, 1996; King, 2006; Marivoet, 2006) and therefore it is not a surprise that they come up in the expressions and enactments of young people when thinking about the Games.

In the United Kingdom, although the English flag (known as the St. George's Cross) was originally associated with demonstrations of nationalism, the Crusades, and the Church of England by denoting an idea of 'Englishness', this has changed over the years and it is now the Union Jack that has developed its meanings to be more closely connected with racism and xenophobic messages, such as those of the British National Party (Hussain & Bagguley, 2005; Richardson, 2008; Gilroy, 2013). I am are not suggesting that this might be the case with the participants' drawings, given that some of them are probably unaware of such connotations. Yet, it is worth highlighting the different expressions of and associations with national pride when using either the St George's Cross or the Union Jack, especially against the backdrop of an event in which the English team presented itself as Team GB. What is remarkable in this part of the analysis is the reference to a country, England, as opposed to the United Kingdom, or vice versa, and the complexity involved in trying to disentangle the concepts of patriotism, or rather, national identity, when contemplating these drawings. The fact remains that, unlike in Brazil, as we will see in the next chapters, in the United Kingdom these flags have played a key role in portraying ideals and narratives around pride and national identity in a nation that has historically been represented in different ways in sporting events. Instead of representing the separate nations of England, Scotland, Wales and Northern Ireland, the decision was to have Team GB competing in the Olympic Games as a unified whole, which was a decision made on the basis of a complex, yet new idea of being British, or Britishness, in contemporary times. In this regard, the use of the Team GB acronym has, arguably, resulted in anxieties and controversies surrounding representation of the United Kingdom in the Olympic Games. Such concerns are driven by the historical fact that the nations of the United Kingdom of Great Britain and Northern Ireland have always been represented as separate countries during football and other sporting competitions (Ewen, 2012). Both Stephanie and John's drawings (Figs. 3.1 and 3.2) display the English flag, albeit positioned differently, which has implications for the semiotic analysis conducted in this research. These two participants are from the same school, which is a secondary and sixth form school with Academy status, located in the northwest of London. In Stephanie's drawing, the flag of England appears along with two other Olympic icons—the torch and the Olympic rings—anchored with the following text:

The Olympics represented Britain and I feel made people feel proud to be and be from here. (Stephanie, London, 9 October 2014)

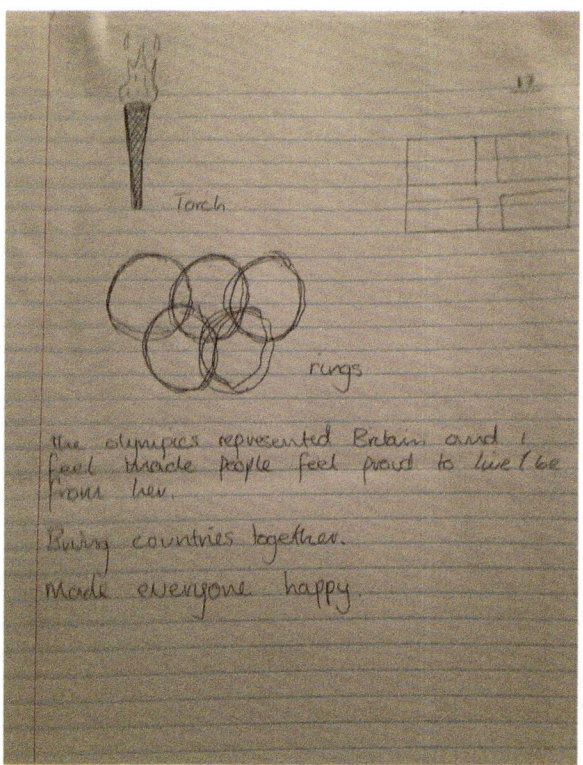

Fig. 3.1 The flag of England with the Olympic torch and rings (Stephanie, London, 9 October 2014)

From a semiotic point of view, the flag should not be analysed separately from the rest of the other elements in the drawing. As an icon, it represents exactly what it is: the flag of England. However, the difference lies at the indexical and symbolic connotation levels of this image. Given the context and the anchored text, the flag of England is an index of the country that is part of the Olympic Games, whereas symbolically, it implies a strong sense of national identity linked to the idea of flags representing countries and nations. The indexical analysis of this same image points to another important aspect. Whereas the flag is an icon of the flag of England, the text written by the participant refers to Britain rather than

Fig. 3.2 The flag of England in the middle of China and the US flags (John, London, 9 October 2014)

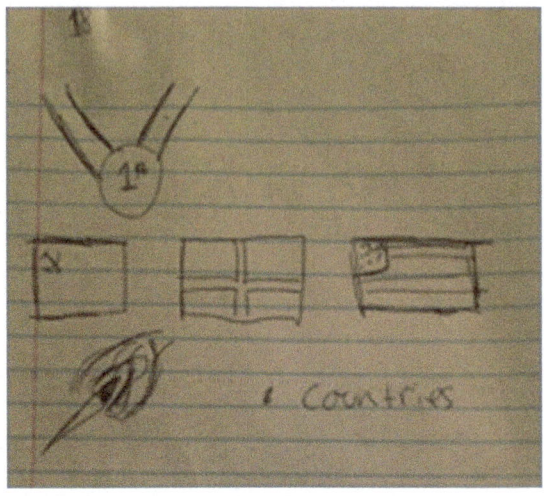

England. This paradox appears in other drawings and texts, which suggests, as I stated before, that participants might not necessarily be thinking profoundly about the differences between the UK or English flags when they wish to express their national identity, nor do they know the differences between the two historically.

On the other hand, the drawing from John sets out a clear distinction between England and two other nations competing at the London Olympics: China and the United States. Once again, the icon (flag) is analysed by taking into consideration its position, which is between the other two flags, and the other elements in the drawing. Overall, the drawing symbolises the victory of the English team over these two powerful competitors at the Olympics. The medal, on the top, with number one written on it, is an index of victory or gold medal achievement.

By comparison, Fig. 3.3 from Mark displays the Union Jack Flag with four people holding hands next to it and the anchored text: 'coming together'. If analysed separately, from a semiotic approach, each of these icons denote different things. However, together they insinuate an imaginary and sociological view of a united nation, including a sense of membership (Anderson, 2004). The text could also arguably be seen as linked to the messages disseminated by the Olympic Industry, such as the slogan 'coming together' which was used repeatedly to promote the Games and thus implying the idea of nations coming together under the banner of

Fig. 3.3 Union Jack Flag, Coming Together! (Mark, London, 22 January 2014)

one sporting event. The general tone of this drawing suggests that the idea of being part of such a spectacular event is a significant opportunity for the United Kingdom and its citizens, including the young person who drew it. As a result, the drawing also exudes a message of pride and patriotism in relation to the Games.

Similarly, Fig. 3.4 also from Mark shows a drawing of the United Kingdom in the context of the entire globe, displayed alongside unidentifiable flags from other countries, but with a magnifying glass aimed at the UK map. The United Kingdom was indeed at the centre of global attention in 2012 for hosting the Olympic Games. Some participants even referred to it as an imagined national community connected to patriotic or national sentiments in light of the Games. Mario, for example, is one of the young participants who describes the extent to which, how and why he felt very proud about the fact that the Games were taking place in Great Britain after such a long time. According to him, 'it was a showcase for what Britain is all about', which insinuates a strong attachment to the nation from this participant.

Fig. 3.4 The United Kingdom through magnifying glasses (Mark, London, 22 January 2014)

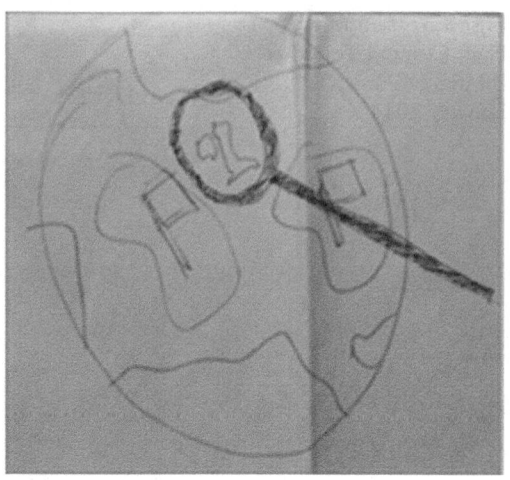

Yet, not all performances of national identity are fixated on the view of being English or British. As a multicultural society, the United Kingdom, and in particular London, is formed out of a plethora of ethnicities and nationalities. The framework presented in this book aims to embrace inclusivity and enable different voices and enactments of identity to surface. The following two examples are from the mind-map exercises undertaken with participants from a school that serves the local community in the Docklands area of London, which is mainly of Bangladeshi origin. As we will be able to see, these two discursive performances recount national identities beyond the context of the United Kingdom and London (Figs. 3.5 and 3.6).

Both Abir and Haresh are British citizens but with Bangladeshi origins. In their mind maps, they opted to use more words instead of drawings to express their remembrances of the Games. The list of words brings up different topics that demonstrate feelings of belonging both within the United Kingdom and Bangladesh. In Abir's mind map, multiple references are made to remembrances linked to Team GB such as 'Great Britain football team'; 'Jessica Ennis'; 'Nicola Adams won boxing gold'. Nevertheless, what stands out is the declaration that Bangladesh was represented in the London Olympics.

In a similar vein, as part of his recollections, Haresh mentions many British athletes, like 'Jessica Ennis', 'Mo Farah' and 'Murray'. Similar to Abir, the idea of Bangladesh being represented in the Games is

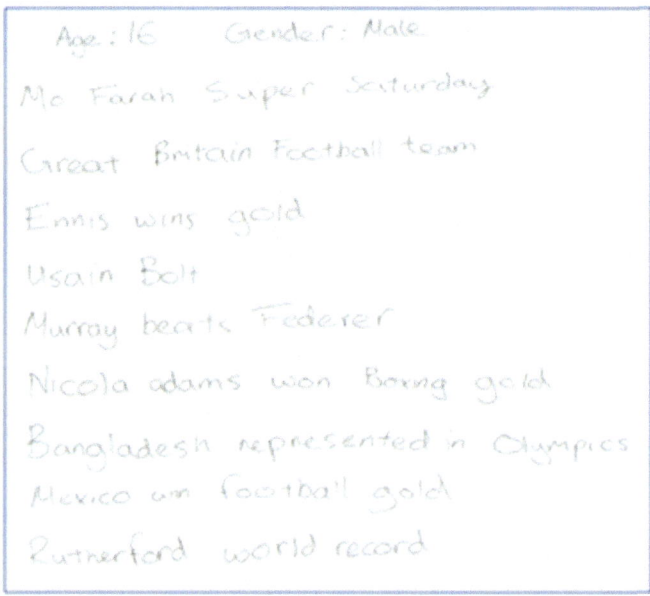

Fig. 3.5 The United Kingdom through magnifying glasses (Mark, London, 22 January 2014)

emphasised as almost an unprecedented fact, which denotes a strong sense of pride and national identity attachment to Bangladesh despite Haresh now being British and living in the United Kingdom.

Nonetheless, sports aside, these drawings are viewed as important symbolic representations of participants' identification with countries. Also, as noted in the case of Abir and Haresh, they may depict multiple identifications with more than one nation, which substantiates the role of transnational memory as part of one's reconfiguration of identity and belonging (Dahlgren, 2013a, 2013b, 2013c; De Cesari & Rigney, 2014).

The drawings also suggest the need to investigate discourses and meanings behind ideals of nationalism or patriotic empathy, particularly in sporting events. Yet, the recognition and remembrance process associated with these images could also be symbolically related to their repetitive dissemination in the media, which is also part of the empirical work of this study and will be discussed further.

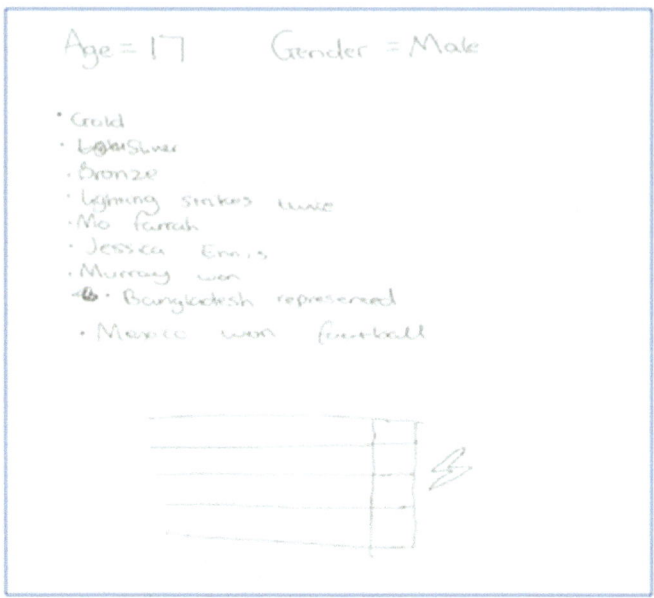

Fig. 3.6   Mind map (Haresh, London, 29 April 2015)

As pointed out by Meusburger (2011), images can and are very often used as a method of propaganda. Although knowledge and remembering are different concepts, they are intrinsically related to and in interaction with each other, especially in the context of Olympic symbols and their meanings. There are many examples throughout the history of the Olympic Games when a particular image of a gesture or action defined the entire Games (e.g. the 1968 Games in Mexico and the Black Power salute from the Afro-American athletes as a way of protesting against racism, and the Nazi salute in the 1936 Berlin Games). To understand the role of the media in the participants' recollections and imaginaries, I draw on the work of scholars such as Meusburger, but not exclusively, in the chapter to come, in order to relate the participants' accounts and discursive memories with the media content circulating at that time.

LONDON 2012 OLYMPIC GAMES: MEDIATED MEMORIES

The research questions initially put forward in this book are implicitly concerned with the role of the media in young participants' memories and imaginaries of the Olympic Games and, as a result, their understanding and performances of citizenship in light of this event. This is because memory and media are symbiotically related and as a result it would be difficult to discuss part of the findings without touching upon the role of the media.

I have previously established the rationale behind the choice of the newspapers front pages and identified the ones selected for the purpose of this analysis. I now outline the key findings from the media content analysis conducted for this purpose. As described in the methods chapter, the front pages of a total of 70 newspapers were examined drawing upon the analytical structure of the following framework for the media (Deacon et al., 1999) (Fig. 3.7).

In the case of the United Kingdom, the newspapers selected were the *Guardian/Observer* and the *Sun/The Sun on Sunday*. Both sets are daily newspapers, with a high volume of circulation, yet are of different formats and political stances. Despite some small differences in the content and structure of the *Guardian*'s and the *Sun*'s front pages, 5 key themes stood out from the textual analysis conducted across the 36 front pages, during the 2 weeks corresponding to the 2012 Olympic Games in London. These were grouped according to the following topics: (1) the opening and closing ceremonies/spectacles; (2) the performance of British athletes versus other internationally acclaimed athletes; (3) gold medals tally; (4) expectations of the Olympic Games; and (5) changes in the city/gentrification.

I draw upon these themes to explain the significance of participants' mediated memories and imaginaries in terms of how these might contribute to their identity performances and understanding of the legacy of the Games.

Most of the themes emerging from the newspapers echo with the participants discourses around the London 2012 Olympic Games as their most memorable moments of the Games, which echoes with the findings from the analysis of the newspapers. I will describe here just a few examples from the data in order to highlight this relationship between the media discourse and participants' views. This does not come as a surprise given that this is a type of spectacle as a central part of the Olympics ritual, and it is known for attracting a great deal of media coverage due to its rich

Stage 1. Position, composition, and intertextual relations	These three components involve the 'formal staging of a news text' (Deacon et al., 1999, p. 174) and the identity of the text within the broader structure of the rest of the discourse.
	Position refers to where the story is located in relation to other stories.
	Composition is about the stories' typographical arrangement and style. Intertextual relations consider intertextuality and the relationship between different stories.
Stage 2 and 3. Sequence structure, source quantity and quality, framing procedures	This second stage of the analysis looks at the text's thematic structure.
	The sequence structure involves the overall arrangement and narrative of the material out of which the news items are constructed. For source quantity and quality, we look at the journalistic sources, the materials, and the extent to which sources may derive from other sources.
	Framing procedures entail news sources that frame and contain other sources, which is common in the structure of news narratives.
Stage 4. Lexical choice	Studying lexical choice involves considering the type of lexicon chosen to support the thematic structure of the text. It can suggest a specific type of ideological belief and values embedded in the text.
Stage 5. Thematic macro-structure and discourse schemata	This stage involves looking at how texts are mobilised in different ways, by examining the headlines and leads and exploring the possibility of broader ideological concepts that are inherent to the text.
Stage 6. Semiotic analysis of images/photos	This is a new stage added to the framework and one that involves analysing the images according to the meaning of the signs: iconic, indexical, or symbolic. To this end, it explores the denotation and connotation meanings of the main images on the front pages.

Fig. 3.7 Framework for the analysis of newspapers' front pages

cultural components (Gold & Revill, 2010). Two modalities were identified within the participants' narratives regarding the memories of the Olympics specifically related to the opening and closing ceremonies. The first attended to notions of time and space, underpinned by the same remembrances. This means that the mediated recollections of the Games prompted the participants to further identify and discuss what they were doing and what was happening around them or in the world when the official ceremonies were being broadcasted. This modality supports Dayan and Katz (1992, p. 212) view that media events, like the Olympics, impose a sense of familialism and create the opportunity for viewers to associate the Games with where they were and what they were doing, which in turn also instigates debate about societal themes. In addition, it prompted them to talk about other aspects of society, fostering critical thinking in relation to the places, relationships, identities and performances involved in that specific period. For Paula, one of the participants residing in South West London, this was exactly the case. Her most immediate recollections of the Games made her reminisce about the opening ceremony which was, in her own words, a 'big deal' for herself and her family:

> *Yeah, I mean, so for me the opening ceremony was quite a big deal for us. Like I remember all of our family got together, well some of our family got together and we all watched it together with my nan. We watched it on her TV, at her house and then we all drove into London afterwards, and we all got pictures on (like) I think it was London Bridge coz it had the Olympic rings hanging from (like) the London Bridge I think it was. But I don't know why it was just (like) quite a big thing because it was the first Olympics that any of my family had seen, so (like) for us it was quite a big deal. And the opening ceremony had (like), so much hype about it and everyone was just really excited for it.*
> *(Paula, 23 July 2016)*

In a similar vein, Hannah also mentioned the opening and closing ceremonies as her most memorable moments of the Games by linking it to her memories of family time together:

> *I think what I found most memorable about the 2012 Olympic Games was the opening and closing ceremonies. I remember watching them with all of my family in the living room, and it was extremely exciting for everyone. My favourite part (as with all Olympic Games) was when the team from each country takes part in the ceremony, wearing their traditional clothing/specially made outfits and bearing their country's flag.*
> *(Hannah, London, 26 July 2016)*

Hannah is a young undergraduate medical student originally from Bangladesh, but with British citizenship. Whilst thinking about the event she is taken back to the opening and closing ceremonies, a moment of the Games that is recurrently mentioned by participants as part of their memories, despite for different reasons. In this case, Hannah focuses on the particular moment that she recalls a family reunion, in the living room. Rather than talking about a specific country, she draws attention to an individual remembrance embedded in a social context, which has been conceptualised as 'a common frame of understanding' (Pfister, 2013, p. 413). In this case, the frame is ascribed to a family setting and a sense of shared feeling of excitement while watching the Games. She then moves on and describes the countries parading their traditional clothing and bearing the respective flags as her favourite part of the opening ceremony. This participant's recollections suggest that her memories are drawn from more familial and local cadres (Halbwachs, 1992), which could also be the case with other young people who were not in the stadium but had experiences similar to Hannah. In fact, sport events, like the Olympics are known for attending to various aspects of globalisation. The opening and closing ceremonies, which display the flags and costumes of different countries, are examples of the extent to which this globalised phenomenon relates to the local level and impacts upon the self-identity of individuals (Tomlinson, 1996, p. 589), thus leaving memories and mediated experiences that can be useful to understand the legacy of the Games in a more familiar context.

The second modality of the mediated memories considers the participants' media consumption, in light of the media analysis previously conducted for this purpose. A substantial amount of data emerging from the mind maps and the interviews relates to the icons, symbols, athletes and celebrities, including acts and performances that were all part of the media spectacle of the Olympics' opening and closing ceremonies. To a large extent, such memories are important because they allowed these young people to reflect upon their feelings and sense of attachment to national identity.

Sylvie's views resonate well with this idea. Not only does she talk about the opening ceremony as her most memorable moment but she also expands on the importance of the tribute to the NHS and children's literature by giving the example of J.K. Rowling, which she understands as part of a patriotic show staged by the host country:

R.[2] In your questionnaire you talk about the opening ceremony as one of the key memories of London Olympic Games. Why is that?

S: Well, I just remember the performances. I particularly remember the beds, children in bed, lying about and I remember it was dedicated to the NHS. Because they merged it with all the children's books that were British.

R: Why do you think they did that?

S: Because it represented Britain. It was something they were proud of, so...

R: They? Do you feel they were really trying to represent the whole country there as well?

S: Yes, it was quite patriotic.

R: So do you think that is positive or negative, being patriotic?

S: Positive, as long as it's not influencing other people in a negative way. So, it's not offending anyone.

Despite the apparent pride and excitement regarding the opening ceremony and its celebration of the NHS and J.K. Rowling, the use of 'they' when referring to Britain, in Sylvie's discourse, is seen as a way of distancing herself from what she describes as a positive patriotic feeling. Sylvie lives in East London, but in the course of our interview, I found out that she was born in Hong Kong. In fact, as a means of comparison with the 2012 Olympics in London, she reminisces about the time when she was living in Hong Kong and the 2008 Olympic Games took place in Beijing, telling us that she felt more part of the Games in Hong Kong than in London.

Another important aspect in the above passage is the idea of being patriotic, which Sylvie perceives as a positive thing as long as it does not influence people in a negative way. The participant demonstrates a sound understanding of patriotism while also drawing attention to the dangers of this concept when used negatively or offensively.

There are multiple patriotic elements identified in the analysis of the newspapers. The opening and closing ceremonies are viewed as displaying the best of a nation that is symbolically and explicitly embedded in the spectacle of the Games. The elements used in the London opening and closing ceremonies are similarly perceived as expressions of the nation itself. Thus, it is not surprising that many of the images remembered by the London participants were partly enmeshed with mediated memories of the opening and closing spectacles. Headlines such as 'Night of Wonder' or 'Golden Wonder' as a reference to the Isles of Wonder conceived by

---

[2] R stands for Researcher and S for Sylvie, the participant's name in this case.

Danny Boyle, brought various references to British icons, such as Harry Potter's Lord Voldemort, the Union Jack Flag, James Bond, Beckham and Mr. Bean, the torch relay, or the Queen. A similar type of rhetoric was identified in the participants' mediated memories, as we can see from the examples below:

Although the above drawings are from participants from the same school, they offer diverse icons and symbols associated with the Olympic ceremonies. In Fig. 3.8, from Peter, four icons stand out from the mind map: the Olympic rings, the torch, a computer mentioning Sir Tim Berners-Lee as the inventor of the world-wide web, and the Queen's crown, alluding to the Queen's and James Bond's famous scene in the opening ceremony. On their own, each one of these icons is associated with a sense of British national and cultural identity. Yet, in this context, they also relate to the London 2012 opening ceremony and a specific mediated memory from Peter.

The following drawing, Fig. 3.9 from Catherine, draws attention to the signs related to British culture that were used in the opening ceremony,

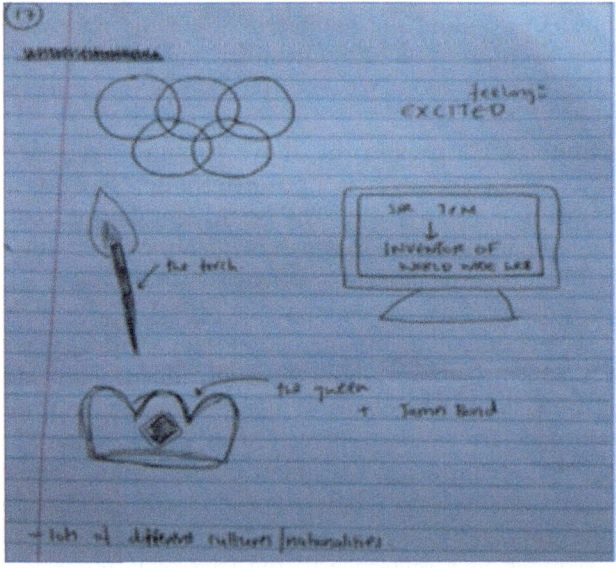

Fig. 3.8 Sir Tim Berners Lee, the Queen and James Bond (Peter, London, 23 October 2014)

Fig. 3.9   James Bond and the Queen (Catherine, London, 23 October 2014)

for example, the torch, and again a reference to the Queen's stunt with James Bond.

All these expressions are viewed as resonating, by and large, with the participants' media consumption. In particular, they echo the content of some headlines on the UK newspapers' front pages at the time of the event. For example, the Union Jack Flag was emblazoned across the front page of the *Sun*, on 27 July 2012, with the following headline: 'Bond, Becks, Beatles, the Baked Bean…Brilliant'.

Such mediated recollections were also a good opportunity to explore as well as deconstruct conceived homogenising views on what is considered British and to further interrogate whether all participants identified themselves with the signs and the cultural spectacles delivered by the host country. Accordingly, some respondents drew on their recollections to compare the ceremonies with those of other countries, while others discussed the cultural aspects of the spectacle itself, with regards to how much of it represented British culture. Anna brought up a couple of important points which, to a large extent, touched upon the topic of diversity within British culture:

What about someone watching from outside this country? That's the thing, it was nice but there was a lot of things that if you were not British you would not understand, and also, I don't think they highlighted the best of Britain. Like, I feel that there was a lot more they could have done ... Such as... I can't remember ... Like there is loads of other artists they could have used, and it is true that people who aren't British might have seen differently. It was very tailored to British people and I get they wanted to highlight Britain and the good things about Britain but you could have been excluding quite a large number of people, you know. Because I think looking at the Olympic ceremonies from other countries they are more inclusive but I guess Britain doesn't have a very much identifiable culture, so yeah.
(Anna, London, 15 July 2016)

Despite being broadcasted internationally, in Hannah's view, the Olympics ceremonies were targeted towards the British population. For her, the innuendos pervading the spectacle of the Games are difficult to follow unless one understands the culture where it is being hosted. As is the case with most host cities, the Olympic Games ceremonies are used to display national narratives (Traganou, 2010). The lexicon used in the analysed newspapers' front pages offers a similar narrative. For example, on 27 July 2012 the *Guardian*'s front page registered the following lexicon regarding the opening ceremony of the Games: 'Time to find out who we are...', 'At stake will be ... what our species is capable of at its best... at stake is [...] people of Britain', 'Olympics will offer the answers to questions that have nagged at us since ...', 'What exactly is our place in the world?', 'How do we compare to other countries and to the country we used to be?', 'The question on whether Britain can actually pull this off', 'A familiar narrative is already in place', 'The Britain of the Daily Mail and Crap Towns'. The above excerpts from selected newspaper front pages denote a nationalist tone commonly used in public events and festivals like the Olympic Games; yet, in this case, they relate to the United Kingdom (Baker, 2015). The choice of words such as 'we' and 'our' are examples of an apparently shared identity and imagined community (Anderson, 2004). Although the Games are claimed as a symbolic medium for the dissemination of nationalist discourses, not all citizens relate to the same sense of community or belonging. In fact, identity is viewed as multidimensional. In this case, different interpretations are ascribed to the idea of being British. Anna refers to this point by stating that Britain does not have a culture that many people can identify with and contests the fact that some of the elements deployed in the Olympic ceremonies may have, in her opinion, excluded some people and other forms of British culture and identity. In other words, the multicultural nature of the United Kingdom, along with the 249 articulations of its past history, presents itself as a challenge when trying to compress the 'experiences and lives of millions of people, over generations, into a story that emphasises certain characteristics and values' (Bhabha, 1990, cited in Baker, 2015, p. 410). The result is, according to some critics, the marginalisation or silencing of certain aspects and groups when 'considering the London 2012 opening ceremony's attempt to narrate a multicultural, multivocal nation' (ibid., p. 412). Anna raises an important point in connection with cultural identity, an area that has played a central role in major political contestation in the United Kingdom. A number of questions remain. To what extent could the opening and closing ceremonies of the Olympic Games be used to elevate multi-layered and bottom-up approaches to culture in order to better connect its citizens with the nation and other cultural aspects? What was missing in terms of the democratic values in the narratives of British history? And, more importantly, to what extent can nationalist discourses, such as the one deployed on the *Guardian*'s front page to describe the event, accommodate inclusivity?

I have provided a glimpse of the mediated memories of London participants in relation to the Olympic Games by linking some of the discourses to the themes that were brought up at that time in the press. I now move onto the discussion of the key findings in Brazil, focusing on the expectations and imaginaries of young people from Rio in relation to the 2016 Olympic Games.

BIBLIOGRAPHY

Anderson, B. (2004). *Imagined communities: Reflections on the origin and spread of nationalism.* Verso.

Asari, E. M., Halikiopoulou, D., & Mock, S. (2008). British national identity and the dilemmas of multiculturalism. *Nationalism and Ethnic Politics, 14*(1), 1–28.

Assmann, A. (2014). Transnational memories. *European Review, 22*(04), 546–556.

Baker, C. (2015). Beyond the island story?: The opening ceremony of the London 2012 Olympic Games as public history. *Rethinking History, 19*(3), 409–428.

Bauman, Z. (2013). *Liquid modernity.* Polity.

Birrell, S. J. (1988). Discourses on the gender/sport relationship: From women in sport to gender relations. *Exercise and Sport Sciences Reviews, 16*(1), 459–502.

Chatziefstathiou, D. (2012). Active citizens and public policy: The example of the London 2012 Olympic Games. *International Journal of Sport Management, Recreation and Tourism, 9*, 23–33.

Cohen, P. (2013). *On the wrong side of the track?: East London and the Post-Olympics.* Lawrence & Wishart.

Cohen, P., & Ainley, P. (2000). In the country of the blind?: Youth studies and cultural studies in Britain. *Journal of Youth Studies, 3*(1), 79–95.

Dahlgren, P. (2013a). *The political web: Media, participation and alternative democracy.* Palgrave Macmillan.

Dahlgren, P. (Ed.). (2013b). *Young citizens and new media: Learning for democratic participation.* Routledge.

Dahlgren, P. (2013c). Introduction: Youth, civic engagement and learning via new media. In *Young citizens and new media* (pp. 11–28). Routledge.

Dayan, D., & Katz, E. (1992). *Media events: The live broadcasting of history.* Harvard University Press.

Deacon, D., Pickering, M., Golding, P., & Murdock, G. (1999). *Counting contents. Researching Communications.* Arnold.

De Cesari, C., & Rigney, A. (Eds.). (2014). Transnational memory: Circulation, articulation, scales (Vol. 19). Walter de Gruyter GmbH & Co KG. de Coubertin, P., 1908. Why I revived the Olympic Games. *Fortnightly, 84*(499), 110–115.

Du Gay, P. (1996). Organizing identity: Entrepreneurial governance and public management. *Questions of Cultural Identity,* 151–169.

Easthope, A. (1998). Bhabha, hybridity and identity. *Textual practice, 12*(2), 341–348.

Eriksen, T. H., & Jenkins, R. (Eds.). (2007). *Flag, nation and symbolism in Europe and America.* Routledge.

Ewen, N. (2012). Team GB, or no Team GB, that is the question: Olympic football and the post-war crisis of Britishness. *Sport in History, 32*(2), 302–324.

Fina, A. D. (2012). Discourse and identity. In *The Encyclopedia of applied linguistics.*

Fletcher, T. (2012). 'Who do "they" cheer for?' Cricket, diaspora, hybridity and divided loyalties amongst British Asians. *International Review for the Sociology of Sport, 47*(5), 612–631.

Gibbons, T., & Malcolm, D. (Eds.). (2017). *Sport and English National Identity in a 'Disunited Kingdom': A 'disunited kingdom'.* Taylor & Francis.

Gilroy, P. (2013). *There ain't no black in the Union Jack.* Routledge.

Gold, M. M., & Revill, G. (2010). The cultural Olympiads: Reviving the Panegyris. In *Olympic cities* (pp. 100–127). Routledge.

Halbwachs, M. (1992). *On collective memory.* University of Chicago Press.

Hussain, Y., & Bagguley, P. (2005). Citizenship, ethnicity and identity: British Pakistanis after the 2001 'riots'. *Sociology, 39*(3), 407–425.

Houlihan, B. (2002). *Sport, policy and politics: A comparative analysis.* Routledge.

Imrie, R., Lees, L., & Raco, M. (2009). *Regenerating London* (pp. 237–253). Routledge.

Jacobson, J. (1997). Perceptions of Britishness. *Nations and Nationalism, 3*(2), 181–199.

Keane, J. (1995). Structural transformations of the public sphere. *Communication Review, 1*(1), 1–22.

King, A. (2006). Nationalism and sport. In *The Sage handbook of nations and nationalism* (pp. 249–259).

Lister, R., Smith, N., Middleton, S., & Cox, L. (2003). Young people talk about citizenship: Empirical perspectives on theoretical and political debates. *Citizenship Studies, 7*(2), 235–253.

Maguire, J. A. (2011). Globalization, sport and national identities. *Sport in Society, 14*(7–8), 978–993.

Marivoet, S. (2006). Part 3 Sports Mega-Events, Power, Spectacle and the City: UEFA Euro 2004TM Portugal: The social construction of a sports mega-event and spectacle.

Meusburger, P. (2011). Knowledge, cultural memory, and politics. In P. Meusburger, M. Heffernan, & E. Wunder (Eds.), *Cultural memories* (pp. 51–69). Springer Dordrecht Heidelberg.

Pfister, G. (2013). Lieux de mémoire/sites of memories and the Olympic Games: An introduction. In *Sport, memory and nationhood in Japan* (pp. 10–27). Routledge.

Roche, M. (2002). *Mega-events and modernity: Olympics and expos in the growth of global culture*. Routledge.

Richardson, J. E. (2008). "Our England": Discourses of "race" and class in party election leaflets. *Social Semiotics, 18*(3), 321–335.

Roche, M. (2006). Part 1 sports mega-events, modernity and capitalist economies: Mega-events and modernity revisited: Globalization and the case of the Olympics. *The Sociological Review, 54*(s2), 25–40.

Rowe, D. (2003). *Sport, culture & media: The unruly trinity*. Open University Press.

Silk, M. (2011). Towards a sociological analysis of London 2012. *Sociology, 45*(5), 733–748.

Smith Anthony, D. (2000). The sacred dimension of nationalism. *Millennium: Journal of International Studies, 29*(3), 791–814.

Tamir, I. (2022). The natural life cycle of sports fans. *Sport in Society, 25*(2), 338–352.

Tomlinson, A. (1996). Olympic spectacle: Opening ceremonies and some paradoxes of globalization. *Media, Culture & Society, 18*(4), 583–602.

Tomlinson, A., & Young, C. (Eds.). (2006). *National identity and global sports events: Culture, politics, and spectacle in the Olympics and the football World Cup*. SUNY Press.

Traganou, J. (2010). National narratives in the opening and closing ceremonies of the Athens 2004 Olympic Games. *Journal of Sport and Social Issues, 34*(2), 236–251.

Triandafyllidou, A. (1998). National identity and the 'other'. *Ethnic and Racial Studies, 21*(4), 593–612.

Wilson, T. C. (2002). The paradox of social class and sports involvement: The roles of cultural and economic capital. *International Review for the Sociology of Sport, 37*(1), 5–16.

CHAPTER 4

Case Study 2: Young Cariocas' Expectations of Rio 2016 Games

Abstract Following a similar structure as Chap. 3, this chapter analyses the data and discusses the key findings of the case study of the Olympic Games taking place in Rio de Janeiro in 2016. However, the discussion is based by looking ahead in terms of the participants' imaginaries and expectations of the 2016 Games before the event took place, as part of their discursive enactments and identity construction and citizenship values.

The data are also formed by two samples, both from the newspapers' front pages and from Rio de Janeiro's (cariocas) young residents' mediated discourses.

Keywords Rio 2016 • Imaginaries • Youth expectations • Olympic Games • Youth identity • Civic engagement • Legacies

In this chapter, I explore and discuss data collected from young residents of Rio de Janeiro who looked forward to the 2016 Olympic Games that was about to take place in their city and the media mood at the time of the empirical work. The data emerging from the narratives is discussed by situating them within different forms of civic engagement within the nation, city and the world, as well as within their multiple senses of belonging and critical thinking about society.

© The Author(s), under exclusive license to Springer Nature Singapore Pte Ltd. 2024
S. Borges Tavares, *Youth Policy, Citizenship Education and Olympic Games Legacies*, Mega Event Planning,
https://doi.org/10.1007/978-981-99-6579-3_4

The narratives of these young citizens from Rio de Janeiro also provide a rich understanding of their own views in terms of legacy, and a deeper engagement at various levels and across different societal topics, which are relevant for policy workers involved in the Olympic Games and any other entities working with and for young people.

The participants' discursive imaginaries do not emerge in isolation. Instead, their expectations and imaginaries are seen as a reflection of and overlapping with their own mediated, personal and collective experiences of past events, which will be discussed in more detail in the section about memory and expectations of the Games.

As we will be able to see from the data, the participants' multiple expressions of identity and views of society often shifted between local and national contexts. Some of the issues brought up by them overlap with enactments of national identity, as they also situate these themes within the historical period lived at the time of the fieldwork. As a result, topics such as class structure, protest movements, the political situation of the country at that time and the role of sports in society, particularly in the city of Rio de Janeiro, come to surface as significant themes for these young participants' own local and national expressions of identity. While for some the idea of hosting the Games in Rio de Janeiro is perceived as positive, others are more sceptical about the positive legacies or impacts for them and their city. On the positive level, as one of the participants explains, this idea is based on a notion of unity and a way of bringing people together, not just in the city or country but also across the world:

> One positive aspect… it's so hard to say (laughs), I guess it's good because we see people watching the same sports from different contexts, so it's about different people but looking for the same interests. There is a certain unification. You discover certain types of sports that you didn't even know existed, like fencing. Like, there is fencing in Brazil? A negative aspect? Well, it does not involve the Brazilian masses and people who really make these things happen; the developments in the city, like works and traffic jams are only going to be used during the Games. After it, I doubt there will be maintenance for the Brazilian people to use it. (Sofia, Rio de Janeiro, 27 March 2015)

Like Sofia, there were other participants who referred to the notion of 'unifying' or the 'unification' of countries and cultures as a positive outcome and a potential legacy of events like the Olympics. The above figures from the mind maps are accounts from two participants from the same school context, Manuel and João, who have expressed similar views. These mind maps illustrate the extent to which the Games, as a media event, is able to transcend mundane experiences (Rivenburgh, 2002) and, in this case, are imagined as a catalyst for bringing cultures and countries together, beyond the national level. However, while the Olympics may be perceived by some, like Manuel and João, as an opportunity to bring people together and to promote other types of sports that are not so popular in Brazil, it may also exclude a large part of the population. This reflects, to a large extent, a sense of national and local belonging when it comes to thinking about the potential of these mega-events. To paraphrase Sofia, the Games are not planned to involve part of the population who work behind the scenes, like in construction, road works and other jobs necessary to make the Olympics happen (Figs. 4.1 and 4.2).

Fig. 4.1 People coming together, a global handshake (Manuel, London, 23 March 2015)

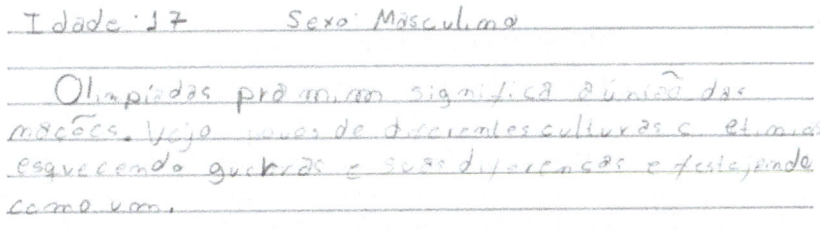

Fig. 4.2 Olympic Games as a union of cultures and different ethnic backgrounds (Joao, London, 23 March 2015). Caption (translation): 'To me, the Olympic Games means the union of nations. I see people from different cultures and ethnic backgrounds forgetting wars and their differences and celebrating as one'

First, the idea of people from different contexts coming together for the Games is an interesting one that contests the underlying class structure rooted in Brazilian society (Santos, 2010). The view of Brazil as a highly stratified society with implications for class structure is a recurrent topic brought up by the participants as part of their own identities and how they relate to the wider public sphere. Hence, class structure, inequality and access to the Games as a commodity are topics that intersect with the different discursive angles raised by the young participants and therefore should equally be contemplated when planning the intangible legacies of the Olympics. Some of these relate to education, consumption choices, lifestyles and access to certain types of commodities or cultural elements that are embedded in different aspects of society. Such stratification, which has its origins in systems of slavery and colonialism in the mid sixteenth century, is claimed here and in the literature to be still visible throughout the country today, including the city of Rio de Janeiro. Despite major structural changes after the country gained independence in 1822, Brazil's social and economic stratification is still highly embedded in the current economic distribution and social disparities that are evident in many aspects of Brazilian society. Some of these differences have had repercussions in different areas, from education and health to workplaces, jobs and levels of income, all of which were elements of concern frequently raised by the participants when they imagined the impact of the Olympic Games on their city and lifestyle. The following headings pulled from the analysis outline different concerns and the debate raised more specifically around the idea of national or local identity, while drawing on participants' expectations of the 2016 Olympic Games.

THE 'REAL BRAZIL' VERSUS THE IMAGE PROMOTED INTERNATIONALLY

During the fieldwork in Brazil, participants asked some random questions such as how 'we' saw Brazil from the outside and what was our opinion of Brazil as a country. In fact, these were relevant questions, as they had a stronger purpose, aimed at discussing other aspects of society that were relevant to them (the participants) and to this research. The participants who took part in the research conveyed a strong awareness of how their country, Brazil, is often portrayed and perceived from the outside, in addition to the role of the media in constructing such notions. These questions were provocative, in the sense that they intended to test if we, outsiders and non-Brazilian, also thought the same as others.

As one of them assumed, 'I know that, when you think of Brazil, all you think about is samba, football, Carnival and bums [...], but we are more than that, you know?' (Henrique, Rio de Janeiro, 23 March 2015).

A great deal of the discourse linked to national identity and belonging emerged as a key part of the analysis. First, the sample of young people who participated in this study were perceived, as connected with, attentive to, and actively engaged with their city and country, which reveals a strong interest and level of participation across various areas of interest. Second, participants were equally conscious of stereotypes created around their country and were aware of the extent to which these issues were accentuated by events such as the Olympic Games. Finally, the idea constructed around Brazil as an international stage is not new for them, with particular regards to other past experiences with projects or mega-events that also took place in the country, such as the World Cup and FIFA Confederations Cup. In that sense, a large part of the participants' narratives were useful to demystifying notions and perceptions about Brazil as a country and Rio de Janeiro as a city. Expressions that compare the country to a 'window for others to see', a 'mask' or 'make up' to look pretty outside are just some that were identified from the narratives and that epitomise the contrasts between the real Brazil and the image that is promoted internationally. Below are a few examples taken from different participants and contexts, which reinforce the same idea:

> I think Rio de Janeiro is being made as a "window" (vitrine) with a lot of constructions and things that aren't going to be completed and white elephants and so on. (Carlos, Rio de Janeiro, 27 March 2015)
>
> Well, you know, Brazil likes to show off a lot to the exterior, to others. This is clearly seen in different phases of our history. For example, with the project "País Tropical", the only changes we saw were in the places where the tourists went. It's a city for tourists. It's like you get to the airport and you have all that publicity. But what happens is that if you come out from the areas where the tourists are staying, then you will see where the problems are. Because my dad, he lives in the USA, and there, they noticed that Brazil was doing the constructions quickly, but what happens is that this is publicity aimed at the outside, from people outside etc. The city of music, for example, it was one thing for us, but how long it took to get it ready? (João, Rio de Janeiro, 18 March, 2015l)

Excerpts such as the ones from above, from the narratives stress the view of mega-events as a catalyst for displaying and improving the image of the country in a way that is often very different from its reality, at least from the perspective of these two young citizens of Rio de Janeiro. João gives us some specific cases of past experiences in which he claims that the image of Brazil was sold internationally, in a way that does not always correspond to the reality of the country. For him, the project 'País Tropical' alludes to an idea that still permeates overseas nowadays regarding Brazil as an exotic and tropical paradise. Such an imaginary perspective of Brazil from the outside has always had an impact on the international panorama and the way other countries see Brazil. Moreover, 'the gaze of the foreigner has played a crucial role in the construction of the Brazilian self-image' (Graeff et al., 2019, p. 798), which in this case has implications for and plays a role in the cultivation of Brazil's national identity. In addition, existing works in this field suggest that the stereotypes and imaginaries created around Brazil, either through the use of clichés associated with exotic and tropical contexts or with negative connotations (see the below an example from Pedro) are, by and large, constructed by the media, in particular the international media (De Rosa, 2013; Graeff et al., 2019; Gutierrez & Bettine, 2021). Yet, João demystifies this idea by contending that such views are fabricated for and by tourists. For him, the reality of the country is totally different from the places where tourists visit in the city of Rio de Janeiro. This means that space and national identity are visibly interconnected in this sense. João also brings up the example of the 'city of music' as another project that took longer than promised to be completed, similar to most projects in the city. Located in Barra da Tijuca, in Rio de Janeiro, the city of music was renamed as a city of the arts when it was launched in 2013. As one of the biggest concert halls in the whole country, the construction started in 2002 and took 10 years to be completed. The comparison made here regarding the Olympic Games and the city of music is made to explain the lengthy process involved in such projects and the implications for the local population that are often impacted negatively by the city works and changes.

Stereotype was equally a topic present in the participants' discourses, who stressed the importance of the Games as a positive platform for deconstructing some of these negative perspectives:

One negative point is that I think there will be a lot of security, but in the long run there will be positive aspects, like showing Brazil to the world. I think the good side is that a lot of countries have a very negative image of Brazil, and this could change. I think a lot of countries think that about Brazil? Well because of the Internet and things people hear, news. Racism things for example, I think often is the media. The games could help change that few. There are good things and bad things. (Pedro, Rio de Janeiro, 18 March 2015)

Overall, the discussion of Brazil's image, both internally and externally, allowed participants to give currency to their preoccupations, feelings, views about their country and sense of citizenship. Discussions about how Brazil is perceived by others were brought up many times as part of some participants' past experiences and, to a large extent, connected with the international media's portrayal of the country during past events. In particular, the concerns raised about how the country is perceived by others, as in the excerpts here, reveal a strong sense of belonging and national identity.

The participants were equally conscious of various stereotypes created around Brazil and the city of Rio de Janeiro and expected these types of rhetoric to be accentuated with the advent of the Olympics. The view of a country where, for example, football is losing its popularity to other sports, such as rugby, is an important configuration in Brazilian youth discourse. Additionally, being well aware and concerned with an increase of the sex tourism industry in connection to these types of events is another example of how well connected, attentive and actively engaged some of these young citizens are with the everything around them. Luis, for example, described how people from Rio gradually became aware of this problem, particularly with the dawn of recent mega-events taking place in the city of Rio de Janeiro:

The other problem is sex tourism. This is a problem, and I think people became more aware of this problem with these mega-events. I have friends, girls, who were approached by male tourists, who offered them money for sex. (João, 25 March 2015, individual participant)

Also identified as a stereotype, with negative implications for the country's image, are the multiple connections between Brazil and football. Contrary to what most people may think about football being a bottom-up, widely open and accessible popular sport in Brazilian culture, central to Brazilian identity, the reality is very different. For some participants, sports such as rugby are starting to gain more popularity, at least amongst the youth population. This is explained by the fact that these new sports are, arguably, less restrictive in terms of practice and elitism, unlike football and contrary to what could be seen from the football industry. Some of these views contradict other participants' opinions who continue to see football as inclusive and very popular in Brazil. The different ideas about these sports demonstrate the plurality of views and perspectives about the Brazilian society that are often connected with class structure and socio-economic contexts:

> I don't like football so much because of the politics, dirty games, racism, and all that. Rugby, on the other hand, can be more violent, but it covers all sort of people; you can be fat, slim, black, or white. It's the kind of sport that anyone can play; you have a place there, and you don't have to pay or be this or that. It's a sport that welcomes all sorts of people. If you want to play, you are always accepted. [...] football in Brazil is not as democratic as people think it is. The selection process is tough, and you need to know the right people. (Henrique, London, 13 March, 2015)
>
> People say that Brazil is the country of football and that football is the most popular sport, but the interesting thing is that volleyball is the most sought-after sport for the Olympics and also the most expensive event to go and watch. So, this means that people are interested in other sports apart from football, and I think that is a very interesting fact. (Mario, London, 13 March 2015)

In this case, Henrique's and Mario's performances link to youth imaginaries, as they challenge and deconstruct national views of popular sports and identity. One interesting fact is that they suggest that football is more elitist than rugby in Brazil. This is despite the fact that people from outside might think of football as a democratic sport in Brazil and might have contrasting thoughts about rugby. Such perceptions challenge how the global and transnational side of sports may reflect different ways of looking at participation and belonging, from the lenses of these young citizens. Whilst globalisation and transnational dynamics are the basis of sports dissemination, the perceptions and stereotypes created around certain national sports still prevail in the public domain, at least in the case of Brazil's football cult, and potentially around mega-events, such as the Olympics. Henrique envisages rugby as a sport that is more inclusive than football because, in his opinion, anyone can play regardless of body shape or ethnic background. Like Mario, he draws attention to the interesting fact that volleyball is more popular than football in the Olympics, which is also a remarkable aspect for him given that football is known for its popularity in Brazil.

Many of the participants in Rio expressed concerns about, and a deep engagement with, the reality of their highly stratified society. This included a strong awareness of the impacts of mega-events on citizens' lives, touching on topics ranging from health and education to gentrification, and in particular concerns about how Brazil is perceived by the international community.

In addition to the above discussions, the analysis of young people's imaginaries, around the construction of Brazilian identity, resulted in more specific topics relevant to making sense of national and local identity. The following sections explore these in more detail.

Local Identity and the Expectations of the Olympic Games

When prompted to talk about the expectations in relation to the role of the 2016 Olympic Games, most of the young participants from Rio relied on previous experiences, with similar events, to express their views about the 2016 Games. Overall, they imagined a scenario where the negative impacts of previous mega-events, such as an increase in crime, corruption and a visible lack of engagement, would be repeated.

Most of the discourse patterns hinged on topics related to youth engagement and the negative impacts that mega-events like the Olympics could have on society. The debate on participation and engagement was, however, connected to other aspects related to the multiple ways young people conceived their city in terms of a public space. As a result, the discussion around opportunities and interest in being engaged with the Games were very much based on participant's socio and spatial contexts. This included the constraints and limitations faced by part of the population when seeking to access events like the Olympics, which reflected the social and economic structures embedded in the city and country. Class was also a topic brought up recurrently by some of the participants as a determinant in ascertaining the level of engagement with mega-events, like the Olympics.

As a result, most of the participants either expected the Games to be far beyond their reach, because of their social condition, or showed awareness of the class structure as a problem that impeded the population's engagement with the event. This idea was brought up across the data, irrespective of school location and the social or economic background of young respondents, which translates into a wider diversity of views from different contexts. Even in cases where the participants did not feel that the existing socio-structural disparities affected their own engagement with the Games, they demonstrated an awareness of how class operated within, and impacted on the opportunities presented to engage with the event. In fact, this related to the fact that only a small minority of citizens in Brazil control a substantial amount of capital assets (Pereira, 1962; Valadares & Leal, 2000; Santos, 2010), as illustrated in the following excerpts:

> I think they [Olympic entities and governments] should allow more vulnerable and needy people to have access to the tickets. I think the tickets should be free. Some of it, yes. Well, the tickets are around 200 reais dude, it's expensive! So, for example, the middle class, not class C, are the ones who could watch some of the World Cup games. (Rodrigo, Rio de Janeiro, 18 March 2015)
>
> [...] and I know that the ones involved are the favoured ones, for example from the higher class. Class C cannot buy that. (Joana, Rio de Janeiro, 18 March 2015)
>
> I don't think the Games have the potential to unite people. I think it may unite people within their groups, but when we talk about class distinctions, I think it will create a wider gap between classes. It creates a sort of line between those who can enjoy and take part in the event and those who cannot. (Joao, Rio de Janeiro, 19 March 2015, individual participant)

Three important aspects stem from the above discourses. The first is connected to participants' feelings about class structure and the experience they have attained, which arose partly from their previous experiences of previous mega-events. As Rodrigo points out, during the World Cup, only those from the middle class were able to watch the World Cup in the stadium. The second point contests the idea that the Olympics is an event that unites people from different classes, unlike what others have said. For Luis such an idea is a myth, as he claims that the Games may unite people but within the same groups. In terms of class differences, he does not see the Games as generating much of an impact. The last and perhaps most significant aspect relates to purchasing power. There is a fixed idea that people from Class C, known as the working class in Brazil, are not able to participate and be engaged with the Games in the same way as people from the middle class. These disparities are seen to have an impact on how citizens feel about the Olympic Games while at the same time also serve to reproduce the inequalities already embedded in the city of Rio de Janeiro.

The idea of disengagement is therefore, in the case of Brazil, entrenched in the historical and arguably colonial contexts of the country. As a result of the rooted stratification and stark inequalities noted in income and urbanisation, class structure is more very perceptible for the Brazilian participants. This is also reflected in the fact that, in Rio de Janeiro, favelas represent a large percentage of inhabitants who are living under the 'myth of marginality' as a set of pejorative ideas and 'attitudes of outsiders towards the favelas' (Perlman, 1976, p. 94). Hence, some young people are aware of how the opportunities and the level of engagement with society are conditioned by social strata:

> *I think it [the Games] should be more focused on the people who live in the favelas; normally, the kind of people who participate in the games are the ones with money, so we feel isolated. (Soraia, Rio de Janeiro, 13 March 2015)*

Soraia is a participant from a community centre located in Niteroi, a municipality of Rio de Janeiro. The aim of this community is to promote media literacy for young people to engage with society through the use of technologies and online platforms. It is not surprising though that Soraia and her colleagues' expectations of the 2016 Olympics were mainly based on personal experiences but also a reflection of their socio-economic contexts. Such perspectives involve the opportunities they have in their local communities and how they recall other similar events that have taken place in Rio de Janeiro. The following example from mind maps, conducted with this group, reveal a view of a city divided by class-based and economic inequalities. In this particular drawing, the participant project his engagement with the Games by connecting it to their own personal economic and social context (Fig. 4.3).

As Pedro puts it, there are the one with money, the 'rich', and, on the other hand, those without money, the 'poor'. Pedro also imagines that some people, particularly those from more disadvantaged or socially deprived backgrounds, like him, may not have the same level of involvement with the Games when compared to those young people living in other parts of the city. For example, in the south part of Rio, which is considered to be a more affluent and middle-class area.

Fig. 4.3 The Games and social inequality in Rio de Janeiro (João, Rio de Janeiro, 23 March 2015)

Yet, based on his experiences of past events, he believes that it will be more difficult for him to get involved in the Olympics than for other young citizens in Rio. It can be inferred from the data that the degree of engagement and participation in the Games does not solely relate to the economic opportunities of these participants. It is also linked to the social and geographic context of each participant. In this particular case, Peter, who lives in a favela, sees his chances of getting involved reduced also because of his local area. Although many young people expect that they may not be able to go to the stadium and watch the Games, there is something else pervading their level of involvement with the Olympic Games, which is the distinct social and spatial contexts of the city of Rio de Janeiro. In fact, for some of these young inhabitants, the Games are expected to accentuate some of the existing problems in their local communities.

Cristina is another resident of Niteroi who goes to the same youth club as Pedro. Although she reiterates her colleagues' views about the fact that the Games are not as accessible for them as for other young people in the same city, she also brings up all the problems that events like these can have for her and her community. Some of these problems, for example, include more deaths in the favelas and young people being out of school due to the Games (Fig. 4.4).

In particular, Cristina goes as far as to describe the relationship between some young people and the Olympic Games as a 'platonic love affair', which translates into one of the many imaginaries of the 2016 Rio Games based on previous events of a similar nature. According to her, if she was given the opportunity to be more involved, she would not hesitate to participate. Yet, in a different way, she also points out a number of problems that would be a result of these events in the city. The expression of 'a love affair' stood out during a conversation with this young participant after I noted that she had written it in her mind map. This phrase was the first thing that came into her mind when she thought of the Olympics. When probed about what she meant by platonic love, she clarified:

> *You know that sort of love, the boy in the school you like, but you know that it will never be possible because he's out of your league? Well, it's that kind of feeling. (Cristina, Rio de Janeiro, 23 March 2015)*

She then explains why she thought that events like the World Cup or the Olympics are normally seen from a distance, at least for her, as she had that previous experience with other mass media events, e.g. the World Cup and the Confederations Cup.

Besides class structure, the socio-economic and geographic context, and the different levels of engagement, or opportunities available for the youth, the young people had generally negative expectations of the 2016 Games. They imagined the Games as such because of past experiences, sometimes first-hand, other times second-hand and mediated. A large

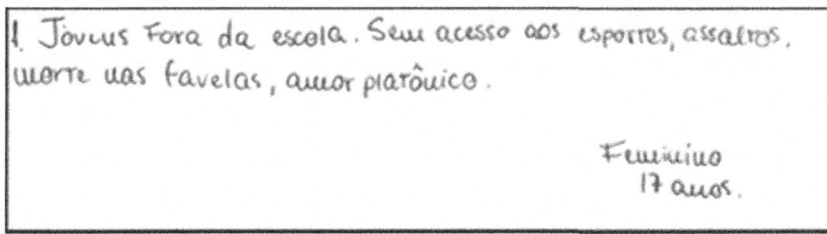

Fig. 4.4 Platonic Love (Cristina, Rio de Janeiro, 23 March 2015). Translation: Young people out of school and without classes. Without access to sports, robberies, deaths in the favelas, platonic love

number of the issues raised by participants were seen to affect the local population before and during the Games. This is best described by Cesaltina, who explained that:

> [...] with the arrival of so many people and tourists in Rio de Janeiro, the buses will be busy and transports full; there will be confusion and problems, fights, deaths, accidents... This is because there is not much public security, only for famous athletes. (Cesaltina, Rio de Janeiro, 27 March 2015)

Similar to other participants from Rio de Janeiro, Cesaltina's expectations of the Olympic Games were very much based on previous experiences she had had with other past events, which in itself explains how past experiences should be taken into consideration when looking ahead at new events and people's. Security was a topic identified as a key issue, especially for the local population, and was arguably one of the most important concerns elevated by the participants in relation to the city of Rio de Janeiro already visible before hosting the 2016 Olympic Games. In addition to being considered a buzzword in the bidding process for the Olympics, the increase in security is not only a rhetorical approach adopted by governments. According to Gaffney, the security apparatuses that have become 'one of the defining features of global-mega events effectively privatize public spaces in the city, installing surveillance mechanisms that continue operating long after the Games are over' (Gaffney, 2010, p. 23).

The participants related to the topic of security in two ways. The first is the geographic and social context of each participant, meaning that location had its own complexities or levels of safety, which undoubtedly has a direct impact upon their views and experiences of security. The second is their understanding of how security operates within the city and the additional problems associated with these mega-events. The latter is a topic that urban and media scholars have addressed recurrently in relation to the city's social disparity and urban structures (Steinbrink, 2013; Bailey et al., 2017), but little is known from the perspective of the impact of the Olympic Games and its legacies. Even for those participants who live in what is considered to be the best part of the city, security is a transversal and critical issue within the city and one that should not be overlooked, according to them. For those living in less affluent areas, namely in the favelas, or other communities outside what is considered as good residential areas, the overall feel was that they were confined by the city's socio-spatial dynamic. This is especially the case in locations where crime and security are more imminent, notably when participants have to commute to school or work. With the advent of the Games, such problems are accentuated due to the highly uneven developments in the city. In other words, and as some participants mentioned before, the Games brought an investment of police forces and other security measures, as well as some other social projects for young people, instead of focusing on education or investing in public works (Gaffney, 2010, p. 26). Hence, despite the social and spatial context, crime, robberies and turmoil in the city were topics with a significant presence, both implicitly and explicitly in young cariocas' discourses, in light of their imaginaries and expectations ahead of the 2016 Games (Figs. 4.5 and 4.6).

The above mind maps reflect, to a certain extent, the claims previously made in relation to how participants construct and make sense of their societal problems. In this case, the participants identify how levels of crime and security intensify during the Olympic Games. This discussion comes up as part of the participants' imaginaries but is also very much entrenched in their specific past experiences or social contexts within the city. The three mind maps come from participants from the same school, which is

Fig. 4.5 Man shooting a woman (Gabriela, Rio de Janeiro, 27 March 2015)

Idade: 16 anos
feminino

Bagunça, assaltos

Fig. 4.6 Confusion and robberies (Sofia, Rio de Janeiro, 27 March 2015)

located in the centre of the city of Rio de Janeiro. These young inhabitants argue that they had to cope with some of the problems created by previous mega-events, which were apparently more visible in this part of the city and in their local neighbourhoods. These issues came up as part of their recollections of other mega-events, such as the World Cup and expectations of the Olympic Games.

> *During the World Cup, we could not buy anything as things were extremely expensive, and the robberies intensified. Yes, during my birthday, during the Game between Brazil and Colombia, I was there in the centre and I sat with my bag next to me, I had my phone and money with me in the bag, and I was robbed. The tourism is going to make things worse. (Sofia, Rio de Janeiro, 27 March 2015)*

These discourses stress the fact that the increased amount of tourists during mega-events is always accompanied by a wave of crime and robberies with negative implications for the local population. Sofia gives some examples of past first-hand experiences when they were targets of pickpockets while the World Cup was taking place in Rio. Mobility is therefore something that concerns these local citizens, especially during these events. It is also a topic that is recalled frequently as significant while imagining the 2016 Olympic Games. As Pedro stresses, the negative aspects linked to crime and an overall sense of a lack of security only increase fear and reduce the mobility of people in their own city:

> *The negative part is that there will be more robberies, crime, like people won't be able to walk around freely, less mobility. It's already very dangerous, so it will get worse. (Pedro, Rio de Janeiro, 27 March 2015)*

Pedro's concerns echo other young citizens' preoccupations concerning the long-term implications of international events taking place in the city. During these mega-events, the planning of security in Rio de Janeiro is perceived as part of a complex history of violence, which is intensified with the advent of the Games. Hence, even though security was a 'top focus and budget priority' (McRoskey, 2010, p. 92) for the Olympics' organisers, such concerns were nevertheless elevated and identified as problematic and challenging for young citizens' urban spaces and their places of mobility. While it has been argued that one of the key conditions for the success of events like the Olympics is 'the security of tourists, visitors, participants and residents' (Baasch, 2012, p. 103), the effects on urban developments and mobility during past events is recalled and brought forward as an issue for these participants.

POLITICAL ENGAGEMENT

Another point brought up by Rio participants related to the economic and political situation of the country, which had a significant impact in how these young people imaged future events like the Olympics. One of the topics of contestation from the past was the idea of hosting the World Cup in Brazil, which drew attention to some inhabitants who criticised the costs involved in the refurbishment of the Maracanã stadium, the lack of investment in the health and education sectors by the government, and the relocation of people for the sake of such events. Although sports, in particular football, have always played an important part in Brazilian national and cultural identity, the introduction of globalised mega sporting events, like the World Cup (2014) and the Olympics (2016), appeared to challenge such a preconceived image. For some of these young people, other important aspects of Brazilian society were equally relevant but seemed to be overlooked by policy makers and governments, for the sake of sporting events and national exposure. Part of their discourse suggested that a thorough consultation with the youth population in relation to the planning was lacking, and this was key prior to the event. Although this point connects to the previous argument about representation and the fact that the Games appeared to be used to present a certain version of the country, very different than the lived realities of many young Brazilians, there are still other aspects that could be improved ahead of the Games.

For Catarina, who lives in a favela, consultation with the location population is something that she would certainly be happy to be engaged as part of a youth community that organises the Olympics. Amongst different ideas, she proposes that students across different backgrounds should pay less to attend the Games. In fact, this is an idea that is also shared by other participants from different walks of life. Yet, expressions of political awareness and engagement with the city or society come up in different ways, often beyond the local context of these citizens. One of the aspects that establishes a correlation between a sense of civic duty and awareness of the political situation is the way some young people envisage the Games. For Sara, the Olympics could certainly be an opportunity for political change:

> *This is an opportunity for them to try to improve, but whether they will achieve that or not, I don't know. There will be a chance to improve the country but we need to wait and see. Whom that depends on? The President. Ah, but in that case it should be another Getulio Vargas. Yes, he would probably be better, at least from the way history talks about him. (Sara, Rio de Janeiro, 23 March 2015)*

Sara feels that such changes depend greatly on the current president. This level of engagement is also visible when participants connect their imaginaries to the current situation of the country, which could be explored in more detail as part of the civic engagement with politics as a consequence of the Games. Alternative political participation, like the one from this young girl, is growing amongst the youth in ways that may not be perceived as traditionally recognised but nevertheless is still legitimised within their own conception of youth citizenship (Buckingham, 1999; O'Toole, 2003; Banaji & Buckingham, 2009; Jenkins, 2011).

Patricia is one of the young people interviewed who is of the opinion that mega-events like these ones are aimed only at part of the population, particularly at those that she describes as the 'panelas', meaning a group of privileged people. She implies something else beyond the structural dimension and planning of mega-events. She views political and cultural representation in Brazil as something that is not representative of the entire population but rather hegemonic and partial, which is problematic for those who are organising the event.

The various existing social projects aimed at the younger population are seemingly seen by some of the participants as initiatives without continuity. Or them, the majority of these social programmes are connected to the city and events that take place locally, such as but not exclusively sports. In the case of Brazil, for example, some of the participants contest the idea of football as the most common and popular sport across the spectrum (see the next sub-heading). Nevertheless, sport, in general terms, is a very important concept linked to the legacy of the Olympic Games and one that is connected to national identity at many levels (Tomlinson & Young, 2006; Smith & Porter, 2013).

Rio 2016 Olympic Games: Mediated Expectations

Similar to what was done in the study of London 2012, a media analysis of newspapers from Brazil was also conducted in order to establish a correlation between the media 'mood' and the participants' narratives in relation to their expectations of the Games. I followed the same framework for the analysis of newspaper front pages (see Fig. 3.7). The front pages analysed in this case were from newspapers the *Globo* and *Extra*, in the two weeks ahead of the empirical work. The following four themes emerged from the analysis: (1) the political situation of the country; (2) the economic situation of the country; (3) corruption; (4) Rio de Janeiro's transformation and anniversary. All these themes were, to a large extent, embedded in the participant's discourses on their expectations and imaginaries of the Games. I provide a few examples in order to illustrate this correlation between the media mood and some of the participants' enactments. An example is the state of the political situation in the country which led some young people to talk about how they felt regarding these experiences, both mediated and sometimes in first-person. Josefine is a young citizen of Rio who is of the view that the political situation of the country is not conducive to making people feel patriotic or in favour of hosting the Games. She draws upon a recent episode in which various TV presenters from other countries apparently mocked Brazil and President Dilma. For this young participant, this is symptomatic of Brazilians' lack of patriotism and she thinks that the ways citizens imagine the Games are connected to their level of satisfaction with the government:

> *[…] last time Dilma spoke on TV we felt that other countries saw it as a joke. I saw this on the media, various TV presenters making fun of our country. The country could be better but because of governments things aren't better. Yeah, I think we are somewhat patriotic but one thing is the country and another is the government. We are very unhappy with the government. (Josefine, Rio de Janeiro, 23 March 2015)*

Others referred to their mediated experiences and expectations of the Games in light of the economic situation of the country and how such events were not beneficial. Like Carlos, for example, who felt that the country was not prepared, economically, to host the Games:

> *I think that given the political, social and economic context I feel that we are after something we cannot afford to have right now, you know what I mean? (Carlos, Rio de Janeiro, 27 March 2015, School L).*
>
> *Before with Carnival it [the cost of living] was more controlled and normal, but now especially with the works and constructions they are making a lot of things that are affecting the environment and things are becoming more expensive, so with the mega events things in fact became more expensive. A lot more. We are suffering a lot. (Pedro, Rio de Janeiro, 27 March 2015)*

Sofia adds to Carlos' view that real estate speculation is a result of the recent mega-events and subsequent developments in the city and again the Games would only accentuate this negative scenario, according to her:

> *I think there are many negative points, actually. But what is happening (with real estate speculation) and the lifestyle/cost of living in Rio de Janeiro is very high. You get to a point when you don't know what to buy because with 100 reais you can't take much from the supermarket and the salaries are not high either. And you pay rent in a bad area which is still expensive. Imagine living here (in the city centre). My friends who live in Europe, when they visit and come back,*

right now in January one of them who was visiting and lives in Germany, another one from Barcelona and one from Finland, they realised that things are expensive in Brazil. And they asked how much we earn here, which is a shock to them. I feel like crying. I come to work here every day but I need to bring food from home because there aren't conditions and if I have lunch outside it's at least 20 reais, minimum. -What could be an advantage to some people, like these little stores with food, those that sell food and so on. But during the World Cup they were forbidden to sell. They could not sell, for example, acarajé near the Maracanã. (Sofia, Rio de Janeiro, 17 March)

Overall, these participants do not see the local population benefitting much from the Olympic Games due to the current situation of the country. They base their arguments on previous experiences of past events, like the World Cup, but also on their personal and mediated views regarding space, transportation and cost of living in the city.

The 450th anniversary of Rio de Janeiro was signalled as an important event for the city. Consequently, this topic takes up a substantial amount of space on the front pages of the newspapers. The tone in the news stories and headlines about the city's anniversary is positive, even though it touches upon the main landmarks and urban changes of Rio de Janeiro taking place throughout the centuries. Although the participants did not mention the city's anniversary per se, they referred to other similar situations like increase on road constructions and significant changes taking place in the city in preparation for the Olympics.

These themes are also brought up on the front pages in connection with the Games. For example, delays in the excavations of the metro as part of the city's extensions and improvements for the Games, as well as issues with other construction sites and traffic jams in the city were identified on the front pages in connection with the city's 450th anniversary. These are all, to a large degree, echoed in some participants' discourses when they imagine the Olympic Games.

BIBLIOGRAPHY

Baasch, S. (2012). Event-driven security policies and spatial control The 2006 FIFA World Cup. In *Security games* (pp. 117–133). Routledge.

Bailey, K., Oliver, R., Gaffney, C., & Kolivras, K. (2017). Negotiating "new" narratives: Rio de Janeiro and the "media geography" of the 2014 FIFA World Cup. *Journal of Sport and Social Issues, 41*(1), 70–93.

Banaji, S., & Buckingham, D. (2009). The civic sell: Young people, the internet, and ethical consumption. *Information, Communication & Society, 12*(8), 1197–1223.

Buckingham, D. (1999). Young people, politics and news media: Beyond political socialisation. *Oxford Review of Education, 25*(1–2), 171–184.

De Rosa, G. (2013). The development of the tourist imagery of Brazil in between stereotypes and clichés. In *Tourism and tourist promotion around the world: A linguistic and socio-cultural perspective* (pp. 21–30).

Gaffney, C. (2010). Mega-events and socio-spatial dynamics in Rio de Janeiro, 1919–2016. *Journal of Latin American Geography, 9*(1), 7–29.

Graeff, B., Monteiro Gutierrez, D., Sardá, T., Bretherton, P., & Bettine, M. (2019). Capable, splendorous and unequal: International media portrayals of Brazil during the 2014 World Cup. *Third World Quarterly, 40*(4), 796–814.

Gutierrez, D., & Bettine, M. (2021). The international journalistic coverage of the Rio de Janeiro Olympic Games: Analysis by media framing. *Sport in Society, 25*(1), 181–196.

Jenkins, R. (2011). *The first London Olympics: 1908.* Hachette UK.

McRoskey, S. R. (2010). Security and the Olympic Games: Making Rio an example. *Yale Journal of International Affairs, 5,* 91.

O'Toole, T. (2003). Engaging with young people's conceptions of the political. *Children's Geographies, 1*(1), 71–90.

Pereira, L. B. (1962). The rise of middle class and middle management in Brazil. *Journal of Inter-American Studies, 4*(3), 313–326.

Perlman, J. E. (1976). *The myth of marginality: Urban poverty and politics in Rio de Janeiro.* University of California Press.

Rivenburgh, N. K. (2002). The Olympic games: Twenty-first century challenges as a global media event. *Sport in Society, 5*(3), 32–50.

Santos, J. A. F. (2010). Comprehending the class structure specificity in Brazil. *South African Review of Sociology, 41*(3), 24–44.

Smith, A., & Porter, D. (2013). Introduction: Adrian Smith and Dilwyn Porter. In *Sport and national identity in the post-war world* (pp. 8–16). Routledge.

Steinbrink, M. (2013). Festifavelisation: Mega-events, slums and strategic city-staging–the example of Rio de Janeiro. *DIE ERDE–Journal of the Geographical Society of Berlin, 144*(2), 129–145.

Tomlinson, A., & Young, C. (Eds.). (2006). *National identity and global sports events: Culture, politics, and spectacle in the Olympics and the football World Cup.* SUNY Press.

Valadares, S. M., & Leal, R. P. (2000). Ownership and control structure of Brazilian companies. Available at SSRN 213409.

CHAPTER 5

Conclusion and Future Pointers from the Lessons Learned

Abstract This chapter provides a final summary of the discussion points presented in the previous chapters by claiming that although young people are already actively engaged with their societies, there is a huge potential of the intangible legacies of mega-events, such as the Olympic Games, that has not been explored in greater detail by policymakers and organisers when considering the Olympic Games and its impact on youth citizenship. It also stresses that the discourse around legacy, particularly regarding intangible legacies, needs to be closely linked to each and different society, settings and local contexts that are aimed at within legacy planning.

The chapter traces, compares and identifies synergies as lessons learned from the two global-divide settings used in the study and ends by providing some important pointers for future research and work for policymakers focused on youth, mega-events and citizenship. Finally, the chapter also summarises the idea puts forward about new framework for thinking about the intangible legacies of mega-events and its implications on the youth population.

Keywords Intangible legacies • Global identity • Olympics Games • Policy-making • Youth policy work • Mega-events

© The Author(s), under exclusive license to Springer Nature Singapore Pte Ltd. 2024
S. Borges Tavares, *Youth Policy, Citizenship Education and Olympic Games Legacies*, Mega Event Planning,
https://doi.org/10.1007/978-981-99-6579-3_5

This book brings together the two case studies (London 2012 and Rio 2016 Summer Olympic Games) and highlights, in general terms, some of the parallels identified between the mnemonical discourses of London and Rio participants based on the excavation of their memories and imaginaries of the Olympic Games. Some of the links established between the respondents from these two cities are important to understand the role of the Olympic Games and its legacies from the perspective of these young citizens, in spite of their distinct socio-economic contexts. This includes the importance of the educational and cultural policies and programmes put into actions for the sake of the Olympic Games in these cities and how it reflects upon citizenship values. For example, one of the key findings from the data is that the regeneration process resulting from global mega-events like the Olympics generates, if not accentuates, the current social upheaval, which ultimately has implications at a citizenry level. At this level, I argue that policy makers working on the programmes and legacy plans of such events need to carefully consider the socio and economic contexts, as well as the possible outcomes, in order to avoid accentuating the existing problems.

These events are also seen to benefit the middle and upper classes, despite each context's different class and economic structures. In a similar vein, the idea of the Games as an opportunity to represent the best of a country or its culture was challenged by many of the young participants from both settings and was often seen as a contradiction of the reality of their respective settings. Their own ways of acting as citizens and the reality of their daily lives are, by and large, distorted from the aims of the Olympic Games values and legacies. To that end, questions about national, local and transnational identity emerged as critical for making sense of the respondents' feelings and performances of civic engagement with a global mediatised event, suggesting that consultation prior to the event is paramount in order to address all these aspects. Particularly for communities whose views and collective reimagination of their settings are key to understand some aspects like regeneration and intangible legacies of such events (Stevenson, 2020).

The topic of sports was brought up in both contexts as an important element (within the memories and imaginaries) both in relation to education and cultural legacies, to further debate other aspects related to national and local identity and stereotypes about access to the practice of specific sports. This aspect is viewed as an opportunity to work with young people on their views of sports participation but also other activities

Games-related, such as volunteering projects and improvement of some sporting facilities. Aside from the synergies identified within these two global north-south cities, many aspects were particular to each setting and therefore key to make sense of the policy strategies adopted in each context in light of citizenship actions. These specificities from both settings are important to note as they are claimed as often overlooked by policymakers and governments involved in the planning of events like the Olympics and beyond, in relation to how citizenship is conceptualised and developed for the young citizens.

Some of the contrasting yet interesting topics that emerged from the recollections and imaginaries of the Brazilian respondents were focused on the negative side of the Games in terms of crime and chaos in the city of Rio de Janeiro and the implications for the young inhabitants, as they seem to accentuate the existing problems instead of providing opportunities for improvements. The participants also flagged the fact that during the Games many of the schools would close, which would be problematic for those more prone to be targeted by criminals in the streets. In the case of London, however, a substantial amount of the discussion focused on the idols and the multiculturalism embedded in the setting, which was an absent topic for the young cariocas. These aspects are seen as important contributions to new epistemologies of youth citizenship and policy that travel from both sides of the global divide (McFarlane, 2006). Ultimately, the framework put forward in this study offers different perspectives around mega-events like the Olympics, with particular reference to the intangible legacies linked to alternative forms of youth citizenship, which is claimed as necessary to take into consideration when planning and thinking about the impact towards young people. Subsequently to these two events, Tokyo's 2020 and Paris 2024 Summer Olympic Games are symptomatic of that need towards the impact it has on young people. For Tokyo, the idea of youth engagement with the city and the Games began way before the event, with various initiatives launched by the city in order to engage people with the strategy, such as around community empowerment, as part of the legacy plans for the Olympic Games (Kolotouchkina, 2018). In Paris, young people were equally at the centre of the Games' tangible and intangible legacies, with the promise of fostering positive attitudes, such as peace, and societal values and more importantly building a better world through sports (Theodorakis et al., 2024).

Regardless of exploring past experiences or imaginaries of the Olympic Games, both case studies validate the fact that the participants' narratives end up touching upon matters that are considered relevant and current for them as part of a socially constructed model of participation in society (Beauvais et al., 2001). Such topics are overtly entrenched in the socio-economic and cultural backgrounds of each setting, as well as their own personal and mediated experiences, by providing a good model for policy-makers, academics and other entities working on topics about youth engagement with the wider public sphere (both from the Global North and Global South).

For example, questions about the UK versus England representation in sports competitions and national versus local identity performances were brought up as critical bones of contention amongst the London partici-pants (given the multicultural context of the city and the country). In Brazil, on the other hand, participants appeared to be more concerned about how the country was portrayed from the outside. In particular, the Brazilian participants highlighted the stereotypes associated with the country and the city of Rio de Janeiro. The class structure was also ele-vated as a perpetual issue in the case of Brazil with implications for young peoples' opportunities to engage with cultural events like the Olympics. In the United Kingdom, on the other hand, references to better access to Olympic tickets for the younger population were mentioned repetitively in some cases and were not directly linked to the class structure but some-what to capital and purchasing power.

All these points relate, one way or another, to participants' feelings about the Olympics, by expressing distinctive ways of belonging and iden-tity performances across space and time. These are equally important issues to take forward within the broader framework of education and cultural policy research, especially in the context of the Olympic Games Cultural Policy developed by each host country (Garcia, 2012).

Enactments of the mnemonic imagination were heightened in the case of Rio de Janeiro because of participants' past experiences with other recent events such as the World Cup, FIFA Confederations Cup and Carnival. As mentioned in the analytical chapters, the participants also highlighted the political situation lived in the country at the time of the empirical work. To this end, the young Brazilians' recollections and pro-jections about the Olympics were subject to the political situation and other past experiences of similar events.

Although this was not so much the case with the UK case study, as the respondents appeared to be less overtly engaged with the current politics, they were, however, very expressive about other political matters such as the use of flags and the problematisation of UK nations in their representation at sports competitions such as the Olympics.

Given the historical context of each setting, national, local and transnational identity performances emerged as specific and significant social legacies of the Olympics event. The framework provided, in both cases, an inclusive and diverse discursive space for participants' discussions in both settings, working as a public sphere in each context. The data collected from the two settings were deliberately focused on different times, spaces and cultural backgrounds in order to allow for a pluralism of youth voices to emerge and to explore the significance of class and socio-economic positions within participants' reflections. Although the London Olympic entities targeted East London as a legitimate area for regeneration, the sample from London comprised participants from and outside of this area to cover a more comprehensive sample of participants.

Similarly, in Rio de Janeiro, the data collection process was purposely aimed at Rio's different areas and educational contexts to offer the same variety and pluralism of views. This resulted in rich, diverse and conflicting narratives and perspectives across and within the same cities, underpinned by participants' recollections and imaginaries of the Games and subsequent implications as legacies for the young inhabitants in the same city. Some of these aspects related to local, national and transnational matters that appeared to be critical for these young citizens. While for some participants from Rio de Janeiro, the idea of hosting the Games was perceived as an opportunity to unify people from different countries and cultures and was therefore expected to have positive legacies, others anticipated this mega-event to heighten the stark differences between the rich and the poor, to generate more crime and to increase the price of goods. As a result, some of the participants from Rio did not imagine the Games as an advantageous event for them, especially those who lived in already economically deprived areas. In essence, they expected the event to bring more transport chaos and to increase the cost of living.

Expressions of discontent about socio-economic issues were less evident in the case of London. Nevertheless, similar topics came up from this sample of respondents concerning the impact of the Games. For example, many participants mentioned the tickets for the Games as an aspect that could have been better distributed, especially amongst the young population.

Other conflicting views related to the role of sports in portraying stereotypes and the repercussions at national and transnational levels.

Football, for example, was problematised in some of these discourses. While for some of the youth in Brazil, this type of sport is still perceived as very important, particularly those from the less economically privileged classes, other respondents saw football as elitist and less democratic than, say, rugby. The idea that others outside the country claimed football as part of Brazilian culture was demystified by some respondents, who stated that not everyone could practise this sport for political, class-based and economic reasons. Some participants went further and described football in Brazil as elitist, highlighting its role in embedding a culture of racism and 'dirty games'. Such contrasting views are arguably rooted in the context of participants' social, economic and spatial circumstances and therefore reflect distinctive views about the same topic. In this particular case, the idea of football being a popular and inclusive sport in Brazil came from participants from privileged backgrounds. One of the respondents was from one of the most traditional public schools in Brazil and known for the education of famous people such as presidents. On the other hand, the participants from a youth club in Niteroi, labelled as who claimed that football was not a bottom-up popular sport in Brazil, unlike what people may think, instead claimed that this sport was elitist and was becoming less popular than other sports. These contrasting views demonstrate that, in fact, place and social background within the same city play a key role in how youth engagement and civic participation is performed in a complex mosaic of public spheres (Keane, 1995). They also relate to theoretical claims around subaltern counter publics and their importance for interpreting different identities, interests and needs (Fraser, 1990).

In the case of the United Kingdom, football also came up during the interviews and focus groups, yet more along the lines of nationalism and the representation of Team GB versus other nations, notably highlighting the importance of flags. In a similar vein, the idea of elite sports was brought up by the London respondents in connection with the Games. For some respondents, the 2012 Olympics were remembered as an inclusive event that contested sports elitism. In other words, unlike other sports in the United Kingdom that the participants viewed as elitist, the Games provided what they referred to as an inclusive event for people, families and nations to be united. Overall, the topic of sports, associated with the Olympic Games, enabled participants from both settings to discourse upon societal matters, such as class structure, stereotypes, access and engagement with different layers of society. Moreover, both cases provided a deeper awareness of topics that were more relevant at one level, be it local or national, than other levels.

Various themes and synergies were identified with regard to the social legacies and impact of the Olympics in both settings. These topics and discursive memories and imaginaries offered important lessons to be learned from across the Global South and Global North divide and the respective cities of Rio de Janeiro and London (McFarlane, 2006). These synergies emerged in the topic of gentrification and the impact of the Games, particularly at a local urban level. In London, this was evident from the conversations and data emerging from some of the participants living in the eastern area of the city or near the stadium where the 2012 Olympics took place. In the case of Rio de Janeiro, the same topic came up, however, from different segments of the sampling, in particular from those who were affected by the changes taking place in the city, such as the disruption of transportation, house evictions and works taking place in the city for the Games.

Similarly, identity, sense of belonging and representation were problematised in both contexts, albeit through different discursive means. An important trichotomy was identified across the youth memories in London and was connected with the 'us-we-local' idea in various discourses, especially for those young inhabitants born in the United Kingdom but of other ethnic or national backgrounds and who felt that their sense of belonging involved a constant negotiation. To this end, references to 'us', as in the discourses of the Somalian or Bangladeshi youths, in support of athlete Mo Farah for example, or feeling proud regarding the location of the Games, overlapped with the 'we' (i.e. the United Kingdom) and the 'local' (i.e. the city of London or any borough, such as Newham, for instance). For example, some participants from other ethnic backgrounds drew on their memories to talk about their feelings and sense of belonging. As they discoursed upon these matters, they negotiated their feelings about different identities that are not viewed as fixed but rather fluid and overlapping across time and spaces (Keane, 1995; Bauman, 2013).

The imaginaries of respondents from Brazil concerning the 2016 Olympics evidenced, as indicated earlier, an evident preoccupation with stereotypes about Brazil, not only in terms of sports but also in terms of how the country was imagined and portrayed from the outside. Representation was elevated in some of the discourses by overlapping with local, transnational and national performances of identity and demonstrating engagement with various levels of society. For example, sponsorship was, like in the case of the United Kingdom, a heated and interesting topic of discussion connected with national identity. A large number of Brazilian respondents questioned the importance of national brands and why certain people (mainly younger ones) would rather pay more for international ones.

In the case of the United Kingdom, a similar approach to sponsorship and national brands was identified. In both cases, the excavations of memories and imaginaries about the Olympics unveiled important enactments of national identity and a solid and critical engagement with topics such as branding and global perspectives on economic and social issues.

It was clear across the data from both settings that representation, whether at national or local levels, was important for most of the respondents' sense of belonging. Similarly, in both cases, the global spectacles of the opening and closing ceremonies of events like the Olympics (in Brazil, participants referred to previous events, like the World Cup) were challenged by the respondents and were not seen as representative of the whole population. In Brazil, the choice of singer Claudia Leite for the opening ceremonies of the World Cup was an example brought up and contested throughout the participants' imaginaries, based on their memories of the World Cup opening spectacle. For them, this singer only represented part of the population, particularly what they described as the 'panelas' (a colloquial term for a group of privileged people, often associated politically with right-wing parties in Brazil).

Although manifested through different topics, the participants from the United Kingdom were also concerned with questions of representation and the role of the Olympics in portraying certain cultural aspects that they did not perceive as inclusive. This was specifically the case with regard to the opening and closing ceremonies which were seen as depicting homogenising views of what is considered British. Given that the United Kingdom is a multicultural society, for some of the participants, the cultural spectacle delivered by the host country of the 2012 Olympic Games was not representative of the rich British culture. In fact, some claimed that Britain does not have much of an identifiable culture, suggesting that, unlike other countries, it would be difficult to represent it through the Olympic Games.

All the points mentioned above and discussions of the two case studies were underpinned by the participants' memories and imaginaries without paying too much attention to the role of the media in such recollections or imaginaries. In fact, further attention was given to their first-hand experiences of past events or projections of the Olympic Games with the view to understanding how they related to national, local and transnational identities and citizenship values. This was done intentionally to separate the two modus operandi, with the view to understanding the role of the media in the youth recollections and imaginaries of the Olympic Games as a critical part of the proposed framework. Part of the discourses brought to the discussion in this section may have been mediated, personal or collective, but the aim was to tease out participants' discourses linked to the research questions posed in this research.

Future Pointers: A New Framework for Thinking Intangible Legacies of Mega-events

This book demonstrates how the theoretical framework proposed initially, based on the intersection across media, youth, memory and imaginaries functioned in practice, by analysing a small sample of data from participants' discourses and media content. The methodology and framework applied in this context is argued as one that could be extended and used in other cultural policy areas in the context of youth research about citizenship and civic engagement. As a result, what is proposed is that the same framework is used within other contexts, not necessarily grounded in the Global North–South divide, but as a methodology that allows youth civic engagement from different parts of the world to be examined and understood. As a result, in addition to the Olympics, other world mega-events and spatial contexts can equally be integrated as part of the analysis.

The framework proposed here considers both the mediated and first-hand memories and imaginaries of young people as important elements for reconsidering epistemologies of youth citizenship and interpretations of civic engagement with the world. Although each case study draws on specific temporal directions (London to look back on and Rio to look forward to the Olympics), the discourses discussed here are often situated as fluid temporal enactments that traverse past, present and future situations (McFarlane, 2006) and that I argue as key to contemplate in other studies now focused on more recent events, like Tokyo or Paris, or even mega-sport events taking place in other milieux such as the World Cup.

The study of the role of the Olympic Games in youth citizenship education and youth policy, as contextualised within the two global settings presented in this book, offers new insights into how citizenship and memory studies can contribute to the existing body of scholarship about learning lessons across the North–South divide (McFarlane, 2006) and to developing new approaches towards the conceptualisation of youth citizenship (Bečević & Dahlstedt, 2022; Harris et al., 2021; Mair et al., 2023; Reis, 2020; Roche, 2023).

Furthermore, the concept and acts of the mnemonic imagination (Keightley & Pickering, 2012) reveal, from a theoretical perspective, how both memory and the imagination are inseparable players in the construction of youth discourses and how these two should be taken on board by policy makers when devising youth policies. In other words, regardless of exploring past experiences or imaginaries of the Olympic Games, both case studies validate the fact that the participants' narratives end up touching upon matters that are considered relevant and current for them as part of a socially constructed model of participation in society (Beauvais et al., 2001). Such topics are overtly entrenched in the socio-economic and cultural backgrounds of each setting, as well as their own personal and mediated experiences, by providing a good model for policymakers, academics and other entities working on topics about youth engagement with the wider public sphere (both from the Global North and Global South).

Finally, this book sets forward suggestions and interrogations that can be applied in light of the most recent Games, like in the case of Paris 2024 Olympic Games. In other words, it suggests continuing to advance the ideas discussed here around the educational and cultural programming of the Olympic Games and the intangible legacies proclaimed by the host cities in contrast with what young people desire as deliverables of such events. Both Tokyo 2020 and Paris 2024 respective Summer Olympic and Paralympic Games would not have been possible without the contractual promise of long-lasting legacies as part of their bidding proposal. Yet, it is important to look at what these programmes entail and investigate further how they might have affected young people's sense of identity, belonging and citizenship values. In the case of Tokyo, the body of research indicates that aside from the safety and security measures, due to the pandemic moment, the city was able to put together a plan that linked the event with society and sports, reflected in the tangible and intangible legacies of the Games (Casini, 2022). Amongst many initiatives that took place before, during and after these Games, it is worth highlighting, for example, the Legacy Project—Nanairo Ekiden—whose aim was to address the intangible legacies of the event through the disseminated wishes and hopes, as well as memories, of the participants (Haggis, 2023) as a way of engaging the population with sports heritage throughout the Games.

More recently, in the aftermath of Paris 2024 Games, I would argue that there is still an opportunity to seize the long-lasting opportunities presented by these Games and maximise them for the benefit of the youth population. As some scholars claim, the problem of the Olympic legacies lies in the fact that often the need to continue the work promised during the earlier discourses of the event organisers and the reality is often different from what is planned (Kohe & Bowen-Jones, 2016). Despite the fact that legacies are complex and hard to assess, the Paris Games could not be timelier in terms of the opportunities they present for Parisians but also other citizens globally. The current political instability around the world and in France with the legislative elections offer a perfect scenario, I would argue, to capitalise on this mega-event as an arena for young citizens from all walks of life to participate and engage in different shapes and formats with what Arendt (2013) and other scholars have claimed as an important and active public sphere key for different types of citizenry (Bourbillères et al., 2023; Brownell, 2012; Habermas, 1991). This can be anything from a local protest, expressions of national, local or transnational identity, enactments of race, religion, among other topics.

Legacies can be anything from the emotional construction of the Olympic Games through the memories, rituals and symbols left behind (Cashman & Horne, 2013; Agha et al., 2012), the level of participation and engagement in sports, improvements through new revenue streams and infrastructure built in the host cities, or the development of public transportation. Yet, most importantly, 'legacy' is also a future-oriented concept with great gravitas for democratic societies, impacting their cultural and social policies as well as the various forms of (in this) youth active citizenship and other enactments of civic participation outside the traditional system. The Paris 2024 Olympic Games may be over but this now the opportunity to assessment and continue researching the role of such events on the youth population.

Bibliography

Agha, N., Fairley, S., & Gibson, H. (2012). Considering legacy as a multi-dimensional construct: The legacy of the Olympic Games. *Sport Management Review, 15*(1), 125–139.

Bauman, Z. (2013). *Liquid modernity*. Polity.

Beauvais, C., McKay, L., & Seddon, A. (2001). *A literature review on youth and citizenship*. CPRN Discussion Paper.

Bečević, Z., & Dahlstedt, M. (2022). On the margins of citizenship: Youth participation and youth exclusion in times of neoliberal urbanism. *Journal of Youth Studies, 25*(3), 362–379.

Bourbillères, H., Gasparini, W., & Koebel, M. (2023). Local protests against the 2024 Olympic Games in European cities: The cases of the Rome, Hamburg, Budapest and Paris 2024 bids. *Sport in Society, 26*(1), 1–26.

Brownell, S. (2012). Human rights and the Beijing Olympics: Imagined global community and the transnational public sphere 1. *The British Journal of Sociology, 63*(2), 306–327.

Cashman, R., & Horne, J. (2013). Managing legacy. *Managing the Olympics*, 50–65.

Casini, L. (2022). Sport as cultural heritage. In *Handbook on international sports law* (pp. 671–680). Edward Elgar Publishing.

Fraser, N. (1990). Rethinking the public sphere: A contribution to the critique of actually existing democracy. *Social Text, 25/26*, 56–80.

Garcia, B. (2012). *The Olympic Games and cultural policy*. Routledge.

Habermas, J. (1991). *The structural transformation of the public sphere: An inquiry into a category of bourgeois society*. MIT Press.

Haggis, D. (2023). A reflection on the connections between art, sport, community and Tokyo 2020. *Welfare e Ergonomia: IX, 1*(2023), 39–57.

Hansen, P. (2013). *Hannah Arendt: Politics, history and citizenship*. John Wiley & Sons.

Harris, A., Cuervo, H., & Wyn, J. (2021). *Thinking about belonging in youth studies*. Springer Nature.

Keane, J. (1995). Structural transformations of the public sphere. *Communication Review, 1*(1), 1–22.

Keightley, E., & Pickering, M. (2012). The mnemonic imagination. In *The mnemonic imagination* (pp. 43–80). Palgrave Macmillan.

Kohe, G. Z., & Bowen-Jones, W. (2016). Rhetoric and realities of London 2012 Olympic education and participation 'legacies': Voices from the core and periphery. *Sport, Education and Society, 21*(8), 1213–1229.

Kolotouchkina, O. (2018). Engaging citizens in sports mega-events: The participatory strategic approach of Tokyo 2020 Olympic. *Communication & Society*, 45–58.

Mair, J., Chien, P. M., Kelly, S. J., & Derrington, S. (2023). Social impacts of mega-events: A systematic narrative review and research agenda. In *Methodological advancements in social impacts of tourism research* (pp. 140–162).

McFarlane, C. (2006). Crossing borders: Development, learning and the North–South divide. *Third World Quarterly, 27*(8), 1413–1437.

Reis, P. (2020). Environmental citizenship and youth activism. In *Conceptualizing environmental citizenship for 21st century education* (pp. 139–148).

Roche, M. (2023). The Olympics and 'global citizenship'. In *The Olympics* (pp. 108–120). Routledge.

Stevenson, N. (2020). Having a say? The potential of local events as a tool for community engagement. *Event Management, 24*(4), 435–445.

Theodorakis, Y., Georgiadis, K., & Hassandra, M. (2024). Evolution of the Olympic movement: Adapting to contemporary global challenges. *Social Sciences, 13*(7), 326.

Index[1]

[1] Note: Page numbers followed by 'n' refer to notes.

© The Author(s), under exclusive licence to Springer Nature Singapore Pte Ltd. 2024
S. Borges Tavares, *Youth Policy, Citizenship Education and Olympic Games Legacies*, Mega Event Planning,
https://doi.org/10.1007/978-981-99-6579-3

The manufacturer's authorised representative in the EU is Springer
Nature Customer Service Centre GmbH, Europaplatz 3, 69115 Heidelberg,
Germany. If you have any concerns regarding our products, please
contact ProductSafety@springernature.com

Printed and bound by CPI Group (UK) Ltd, Croydon, CR0 4YY
27/04/2026
02097570-0009